351

ADRIAN ZUCKERMAN
PRESIDENT 1ST. TERM

ALLAN MINK
VICE PRESIDENT

ANTHONY PELHAM
FOOD STEWARD

JONATHAN COHEN
TREASURER

STEPHEN OFSTHUN
SECRETARY 1ST. TERM

RUSSELL KALIS
HOUSE MANAGER

ROBERT MANDEL
ATHLETIC CHAIR.

ROBERT WOLF
PLEDGE TRAINER 1ST. TERM

LOUIS COHEN
CRITIC 1ST. TERM

ROBERT ANDERSON
SOCIAL CHAIR. 1ST. TERM

351

The History of the Startup and First Year of the Lambda
Phi Chapter of the Alpha Delta Phi Fraternity at MIT

Tony Pelham

anthonypelham@gmail.com

First Printing, 2021

ISBN 979-8-4609-0181-4

Cover art by Tony Pelham.

First Edition

10 9 8 7 6 5 4 3 2 1

Acknowledgments

Many people generously gave their time and talent to this project.

I would like to thank those members of Lambda Phi's first two pledge classes who spent time sharing memories and recollections from the earliest years of the chapter – Jon Cohen, Louis Cohen, Russ Kalis, Rob Mandel, Al Mink, Bob Wolf, Adrian Zuckerman, Matt Alves, Andy Bronstein, Tom Burgmann, Bob Glatz, Carl Heinzl, Todd Hubing, Loren Kohnfelder, and Jeff Thiemann.

In addition, I am appreciative of the generous efforts of Pam Thiemann, Mike "Corky" Corcoran, and David Eddy in providing supplemental information about our chapter's startup. And thanks go out to Steven Bergstein, who provided invaluable information concerning the building's lease, the Friends of the Lambda Phi Chapter Board, and the current state of the chapter, and to Ray Tsou, who brought me up to speed on the duties of the current kitchen manager.

Special thanks to those in the first pledge classes who reviewed drafts, and to Dave Jilk for offering much substantive feedback and suggestions.

Preface

"No man ever steps in the same river twice, for it's not the same river and he's not the same man."

Writing a history, even about something from only four decades ago, can be a daunting task.

Inserting my sixty-four-year-old self back into my nineteen-year-old mind results in interpretations and explanations that don't necessarily reflect the reality of every detail from my past. I'm not the same person I was. None of us are.

Generally, we tend to recall events in a manner that casts us in a positive light. We are the heroes of our journey. I don't pretend to be an exception.

I believe that there is a historical "Truth," at least in terms of a historically accurate record of facts and details that have taken place, but there is another type of truth—how these facts and the happenings of the day were perceived by those involved, and how these events affected those who participated in them.

There is no standard by which the second truth can be measured in terms of accuracy, but it can be set to words, as I've attempted to do here, to provide a meaningful window into the process that led to our chapter at MIT.

As part of the process of writing our chapter's early history, I've strained my memory to its limit, and in the process, I've discovered that I have no recollection of large parts of my fraternity experience. In contrast, small, seemingly obscure moments are still vividly remembered—fondly in some cases—not so much in others.

I've examined all documents that I could find from the era that pertain to the events of the time. Some, like leases and statistics, are hard facts. Others, like newspaper articles, or the President's annual report, already contain various degrees of factual 'reinterpretation,' reflecting each author's viewpoint.

I've contacted as many as I could of those who were involved in some aspect of the startup of the Lambda Phi chapter, and who were willing to share their memories with me. I am grateful to all who participated. Each contributed to the collective memory of the events of the day. Each provided their interpretation and recollections of important occasions and memorable experiences.

In many cases, I've recreated dialogue that represents exchanges that may have (should have?) occurred. I make no assertion that the dialogue is accurate, or that it even took place. But it seems to be a far more interesting way of presenting many events than would a dry description of facts.

Many times, after a conversation, we often come up with a much better response than what we actually said at the time.

"I wish I'd said such-and-such."

The benefits of writing a history in which I am a character means that I can accomplish such a feat.

The writing of only a small part of the chapter's history has taken much longer than I originally envisioned, but it would be news if that weren't the case.

The history of each year of the fraternity has fractal properties. It grows as you move from a macro view of the entire fraternity down to each pledge class, and expands further as you move to each individual. And it increases again as the time increments between covered events shrink. At some level of detail, no one cares, even those who were involved.

I've tried to cover most of the history of the important events related to founding our chapter and its first year of operation, at a high enough level that it may be interesting to more than just those who were directly involved.

I've verified the fact that my memories are faulty. Before writing this work, I would have sworn that the bar downstairs was built by Al Mink, himself, in our very first work week. It turns out that he had nothing to do with its construction, and that it was built months later as a pledge project.

It's not inconceivable that a few of my other memories are similarly suspect. Unless specifically refuted, I've included them here.

Most books, especially in today's era where self-publishing is easy and available to almost anyone, are only read by a handful of people. A few select will be runaway best sellers, with sales numbering in the millions. Others will be lucky to be read by thousands.

Most are read only by a few friends and family. But even in such cases, the benefit is in the writing. It's cathartic, it's emotional, it's captivating to be in "the flow," when ideas pour out faster than you can type, and you just hope you can capture enough fragments of them to assemble them later into a coherent narrative.

It's hard to escape the conclusion that the primary benefit of most books is for the author.

I'm fortunate. I have a built-in audience for this book—the four-hundred or so alumni of the Lambda Phi chapter. The flip side is that this is also probably the *only* audience for the book, so it's unlikely to reach the New York Times list.

But the writing of it has given me a reason to get in contact with people I haven't talked to in years—or decades in some cases—people with whom I shared a critical period of my life. It's highly likely, as one brother observed, that we spent more time with our fraternity brothers than anyone other than our immediate family.

Talking with my brothers from years ago never fails to raise a smile—usually a laugh—and was never a burden.

351

Killian Court

We stared out into the Killian Court at the crowd of freshmen, waiting for Dr. Weisner to say, "the words."

We'd carved out a small stake on the grassy periphery of the court, battling for prime real estate with thirty other MIT fraternities. Standing ground on our patch of turf, a few things set us apart from the other groups of fraternity brothers gathered around us.

For one thing, we weren't.

Brothers, that is.

Five months prior, our group had only existed in the abstract. Four weeks later, there were names attached.

However, we were still, at the time, pledges.

The size of our contingent also distinguished us. At most ten men, but actually, fewer, since we couldn't send the entire house, we were, at best, half the size of the next smallest fraternity. Maybe even a third.

And we were an unknown.

"Which frat are you?" we were asked.

As fraternity shirts, colors, and flags were not visible until rush officially began, it wasn't obvious which group belonged to which frat.

"Alpha Delta Phi."

A blank stare was the typical response, followed by slow signs of dim awareness.

"Oh yeah. I think I heard about you guys."

After quickly scanning our scant numbers, we were usually dismissed with a slight smirk.

"Well, anyway, good luck"

•

In the Fall of 1976, fraternity rush occurred during the Residence/Orientation Week, the week before the start of the semester. Representing social Darwinism at its finest, the thirty-one MIT fraternities competed against each other for the "best of the best" out of the 1050 freshman and transfer students in the entering class.

Many fraternities had reputations. Sigma Alpha Epsilon was the "jock" fraternity. Others were "party" frats. One, the "Number Six Club," was coed. It wasn't even clear if they were a frat.

What kind would *we* be?

Adrian, Moose, and I played on the freshman squash team. Al and Jon rowed with the freshman crew. Steve was on the track team. But it was pretty clear that none of us considered ourselves to be "athletes." A jock frat appeared fairly unlikely.

A party frat? That seemed equally improbable, given our current makeup. Bob Anderson was the most socially adept of our group, but Bob seemed more likely to plan an elegant social evening than a drunken beer-fest.

Preppies? It was true that nine of us were from the east coast, but we'd managed so far to avoid anyone who even hinted of being stuck-up. And we planned to keep it that way.

Socially-inept nerds? Hmmm.

Here was a resource that MIT had in plenty. While everyone at MIT might be considered somewhat nerdy when compared to the general population-at-large, the Institute also had a large, dedicated population of what might be termed "super-nerds."

While we welcomed really smart people, they had to exhibit

2

some basic degree of social aptitude.

●

I pondered our group. Each of us was brilliant, in various ways. But at MIT, that quality alone did not set one apart.

Al Mink, from Fort Lauderdale, Florida, was a natural leader. It was clear he would be one of the main officers of the fraternity, and equally clear that he would ably represent the fraternity in dealings with the MIT establishment.

Louis Cohen, a native Bostonian from West Roxbury, took no BS from anyone and felt free to dispense his prodigious wit, in unlimited supply, in a wicked "Bahston" accent.

Rob "Moose" Mandel, from Tenafly, NJ, was equal parts hilarious and insightful. It was rare to come away from a conversation with Moose without marveling at his comic genius—along with his piercing analysis.

Adrian, a first-generation Romanian immigrant from Connecticut, had a unique ability to make people feel welcome and valued. It was abundantly clear he would be one of our most valuable assets during our first rush week.

Russ Kalis, solid and laconic, channeled an early lumberjack vibe. Hailing from Minnesota, Russ was the only member of our group not from an east coast state. If Russ answered a question with more than one syllable, you sat up and paid attention, because something of great importance was forthcoming.

Jon Cohen, from upstate New York, keenly intelligent and analytical, represented the best of the fraternity, intellectually.

Bob Wolf, cheerful and perpetually optimistic, from nearby Newton, Mass, helped to counter any negativity that might crop up.

Steve Ofsthun, from Buffalo, NY, was perhaps, the most well-rounded of the group. Cheerful and whip-smart, he had the kind of welcoming personality that made everyone comfortable in his presence.

Bob Anderson, hailing from Montclair, New Jersey, had a perpetual smile and could charm almost anyone. Bob was the most mature among us and provided a moderating influence on any potential excesses. He had a gift for event planning. It was pretty clear that Bob would become our first social chairman.

And then there was me, Tony Pelham, from Baltimore, Maryland. Quiet and introspective, I might have been the opposite of the stereotypical fraternity member. Small-talk during rush week was not my forte. I preferred to focus my energies behind the scenes, such as getting our building readied for occupancy, and making sure we had something edible to eat.

After all, somebody had to do it.

•

Perhaps, rather than looking for jocks, party animals, or brainiacs, we were simply looking for people that possessed what we might call in today's terms, "emotional intelligence."

But then again, so were most of the other frats.

And it wasn't clear at that moment that we would successfully compete against the already-established frats. Each of them had members and alumni who had years of experience in rush week. Each had a long history from which to build, and each had developed and refined their rush week activities based on past successes. They knew what worked for them.

We were winging it.

We were somewhat confident that students would visit our house. But would there be enough of them? And would they be the kind of people we wanted?

And we agonized over how many bids to extend.

Too selective, and we might end up not filling our chapter house, which at the time was limited to slightly over twenty. That would drive up the costs for all of us, not a desirable outcome. And it would make it tougher to fill our house in the following years.

But if we weren't selective enough, we might not get the kind of people we were looking for. And if we gave out too many bids we could end up with many more people than we had room for.

All-in-all, our first rush was a recipe for mega angst and anxiety, at least to those, like me, who are prone to such things.

Given all of our concerns, I did the only thing that I could. I left these problems for others to worry about.

•

Upperclassmen in the crowd wore their frat shirts covered up by an outer shirt. It was against the rules to display the fraternity letters until the rush officially began. We didn't have official fraternity shirts at that point, again, just some homemade shirts, and a flag, sewn by Al's girlfriend, Sandy.

A whirlwind of activity was about to begin, exhausting for all involved, and when it was over, we knew only that we'd end up with, as Benjamin Franklin might have said to us:

"A fraternity, if you can keep it."

As President Weisner finished his speech, he pointed out towards the assembled crowd and proclaimed the words we had been waiting to hear:

"Let the rush begin!" [1]

---

[1]   https://amp.blog.shops-net.com/6864860/1/list-massachusetts-institute-of-technology-fraternities-sororities-and-ilgs.html

Leeb Well Enough Alone?

The phone's piercing ring destroyed the silence.

"Who is it this time?"

By 1976, Henry Leeb, now 82 years old, was tired. His college years at MIT, now some sixty-plus years in the past, were a distant memory, a distance that seemed to be accelerating at a rate far faster than his chronological years. Recollections about the Lambda Phi fraternity, which he'd joined in 1911, before the "Great War," were rapidly drifting from his cognition.

Since his time at MIT, he'd seen his alma mater progress from a mere "trade school" to one of the foremost centers for science and technological education in the country, perhaps in the entire world.

He barely recalled his efforts, begun in his undergraduate years, to petition the International Alpha Delta Phi fraternity to accept his chapter into their organization.

At the time, Alpha Delta Phi wasn't just any fraternity. They were one of the oldest, and perhaps the most prominent international fraternity in his day. President Teddy Roosevelt, then just two years out of office, was an Alpha Delt from the class of 1880, albeit from the now-disbanded Harvard chapter.

Well, nobody's perfect.

Becoming part of the International fraternity was the sole reason that his chapter had been formed eleven years earlier. He was never quite sure why the Lambda Phi chapter had been so thoroughly, and repeatedly, rejected by the Alpha Delts.

He had a sneaking suspicion that his efforts were being thwarted by a persistent and concerted lobbying effort from certain "gentlemen" across the river in Harvard Square, alumni of the now non-existent chapter, as their once proud Alpha Delta Phi chapter had been shuttered, along with all other campus fraternities, by the University in 1907.

More likely, however, was that MIT was not perceived to be a good fit for the organization's "literary" goals. The only literature being produced at MIT at the time was engineering textbooks. And the only art was blueprints and technical diagrams. Or so, some may have thought.

Henry believed that literary prowess wasn't limited to the writing of poetry and dry prose. The creativity and brilliance he'd seen and experienced from his fellow Lambda Phis and other MIT students, had convinced him that there could be another side to "literary excellence."

Nevertheless, all his efforts to date had proved futile. With his chapter's goal seemingly unobtainable, the goal of a Lambda Phi chapter of the Alpha Delta Phi fraternity at MIT gradually faded away, much like his own memories of his time there. And if it was not to be, Henry had other things to do—like getting on with his life.

•

Years later, in 1961, a most peculiar thing happened. Some five decades after he'd first joined Lambda Phi, Alpha Delta Phi contacted Henry about efforts to establish a chapter at MIT. The roles had reversed. Now, the International organization was petitioning *him*.

While some might have told ADP, after all this time, where they needed to "shove it," there still existed inside Henry a small spark, a never-extinguished desire to realize his original goal. Maybe this would be the time the spark would ignite into a full-blown fire.

This time, however, it was MIT that stamped out his dreams. The Institute was most definitely not interested in expanding its fraternity system. In the late 50s and early 60s, undergraduate enrollment at MIT was stagnant or even declining. Another fraternity would simply take students away from existing fraternities, or the dormitories. Either outcome, from the Institute's point of view, was undesirable.

Thwarted again, Henry went back to living his life and enjoying his retirement with his wife Katrina, now content with the understanding that his earlier dreams were never going to be realized.

At least, that is, until he picked up the phone.

Field Rep

Mike "Corky" Corcoran was a little skeptical.

"Restarting a chapter's one thing. But what you're talking about is going to be, well..., difficult."

The "two Bobs," McKelvey and Price, were on the expansion committee for the International ADP fraternity.

They'd hired Corky due to his stellar work in turning around the Minnesota chapter. The late sixties and early seventies had been a difficult era for fraternities in general. The social revolution of the time had students more interested in protesting the war and celebrating personal freedom than in joining campus social groups with decades-old 'traditions.'

Fraternities were dying.

Already in the past year, Corky had had to make tough decisions to get chapters back on track. At the Stanford chapter, members had converted their jacuzzi area into a greenhouse used for growing vegetation that was especially popular for smoking. The Stanford administration was not amused.

The greenhouse had to be destroyed. And various members had to be "removed" to restore that chapter to the good graces of the University and to make it functional as a member of Alpha Delta Phi.

And it had worked.

But starting an entirely new chapter meant procuring a living space, recruiting a core team, and then growing from there, a process that could take years.

And at MIT, of all places.

Corky's view of MIT students reflected that of popular culture at the time—slide-rule-toting nerds, many probably named "Poindexter," with all the social skills of a pimply teenager still having wet dreams about his first kiss.

That's going to be quite the frat.

•

He'd only been on the job for a year, and the pay was, frankly, abysmal. But Corky had been able to travel around the country, in his green VW Beetle, visiting various chapters. And there were plenty of parties to be had. That was one of the best perks of the job.

While working with the Stanford chapter, he'd been invited to the home of Alpha Delt David Packard, co-founder of the Hewlett-Packard company. David had even shown him the famous "garage" where he and Bill Hewlett had created their first product.

•

"You're not going to have to do it all yourself," Bob Price interjected, bringing Corky back into the moment. "We've got an MIT alum who's been pushing this thing hard."

Corky's spirits lifted—slightly—with this news. Having a prominent (and hopefully wealthy) alumnus would be a huge help.

"He's class of 1915," Price continued.

Shoot me now.

"Wait. He's been trying to get this going for, what, sixty years?" Corky asked rhetorically.

"Does he have a time frame when he'd like to see this thing happen, sometime before, say, the next millennium? To be honest, I'm not sure I see myself in this position for that long."

10

"Well, he's 82 years old, and in poor health," Brother McKelvey added.

This is not helping.

"But MIT is tremendously supportive of their alumni," Bob continued. "Right now, they've got a huge undergraduate housing crisis. They need more rooms, soon. And they have a building for the chapter house in mind. As a matter-of-fact, they own it."

That information *did* help. One item could be checked off his list, already.

"How big is the building?" Corky asked.

"They're thinking it's got room for 55 to 60 brothers," the other Bob answered.

"Is that all?"

That would only make it the largest Alpha Delt chapter in the country. In the universe, for that matter.

"And they need this when?" Corky asked tentatively, already anticipating the Bobs' response.

"They're shooting at getting it going by the fall semester of '76. All they need are a core group to get the ball rolling."

"Don't tell me. They currently have nobody."

"Well, that's where you come in. You're going to be our man in the trenches."

Along with the Poindexters, apparently.

"This thing may take off"

In the mid-70s, MIT had a problem. A money problem. As in—they needed more of it. An article from the student newspaper from February 1977 bluntly explained the issue:

> The institute is faced with an endowment that has not grown to keep pace with inflation at the time that its expenses are soaring. The administration has taken two major steps in order to counteract this trend: cutting expenditures and attempting to increase income and gifts. The primary means of increasing income has been to increase the number of undergraduates. [2]

Thus, MIT's solution to their monetary woes took the form of increased tuition revenues resulting from bumping up the number of undergraduates from 4,000 to 4,400. The article continued:

---

[2] The Tech, Sep 13 1977, v97-37.

12

The addition of 100 students to the freshman class increases annual tuition revenue by about $400,000. The cost of educating those extra students is far less than this amount because no new facilities and few extra personnel are required to educate them. [3]

Only one obstacle stood in the way of this revenue windfall—where in the world, or more practically, where on campus, would these extra students live?

The dormitory system was already overcrowded. The fraternities were full. An article from February 1976 outlined Dean Browning's take on this problem:

"MIT has projected dormitory overcrowding at 150 students next year," Ken Browning says, with "No specific plans for where to put them yet." [4]

Overcrowding meant that many dorm-room doubles could become triples and that singles would become doubles. In the extreme case, students coming from the local area would be denied entry into the dormitory system, and thus would be forced to either commute or to find their own accommodations.

However, a possible solution to the overcrowding problem began to bubble up in the minds of the MIT housing administration, perhaps in response to the meeting held on February 5 between MIT's Browning and Alpha Delt alumni Andrew Onderdonk, Robert Price, and field rep Mike Corcoran. They explained the fraternity's interest in expanding to include a chapter at MIT.

Something must have clicked, for on March 2, just a few weeks later, the Dean noted:

"Other possible plans for easing the housing crunch include the formation of another men's fraternity," Browning stated. "A 'low key national fraternity,' Alpha Delta Phi, is "interested in forming another all men's living group." [5]

It's not clear what was "low key" about Alpha Delta Phi, at

---

[3] Id.
[4] The Tech, Feb 13, 1976, v96-4.
[5] The Tech, Mar 2, 1976, v96-8.

least in the mind of Dean Browning. Perhaps it was the literary aspect of the fraternity or the lack of any huge hazing scandals in any of the chapters.[*]

He continued:

> "The Interfraternity Conference (IFC) has already given permission to this fraternity and formed an expansion committee to assist them," Browning noted, adding that a group of students from MIT has shown interest in forming another living group, "and if they ever get together with Alpha Delta Phi, this thing may take off." [6]

A mere month later, in April, the wheels had begun to turn. Permission for ADP to "colonize" had been approved, a quaint term that today might seem inappropriate in certain situations, but one that's still used when discussing fraternity expansion.

Even with the approval, the Dean seemed unsure if the efforts to start a new chapter could be accomplished in time for the next academic year. As he stated in The Tech:

> The national fraternity Alpha Delta Phi (ADP) has been given permission by the Interfraternity Conference (IFC) to "colonize here," Browning said, but plans "haven't gotten off the ground yet." Browning said that the new fraternity, which would house about 50 people, should be ready by this fall or the fall of 1977 at the latest.
> [7]

Unbeknownst to the Dean, the process of "getting off the ground" was already well underway.

---

[*] It was most fortunate for our chapter that the movie "Animal House" would not come out for another two years.

[6] The Tech Mar 2, 1976, v96-8.

[7] The Tech Apr 9, 1976, v96-17.

14

Not Half Bad

These guys aren't fucking around.

Corky's meeting with the MIT top brass had made an impression. They wanted this thing to happen, and happen fast. They already had plans underway to renovate their old apartment building, and they were so desperate, they planned to occupy it right away, and do the renovations *around* the people living there.

The building they owned was huge—it could hold over a hundred people. Corky learned that the building was to be shared with a women's group.

That could prove interesting.

And he'd met with Henry Leeb. A real nice guy. Leeb had explained to him the whole Lambda Phi origin story, along with his thwarted attempts, mostly by ADP, to affiliate his chapter with the international organization.

"Most people would have given up," Corky thought. "You've got to give the man some serious props for sticking with it."

In his meetings on campus, and his informal survey of the

Institute's dorms and frats, Mike had gotten to see, and talk to, a variety of students.

To his surprise, he'd seen relatively few Poindexters. For the most part, the ones he'd seen looked like normal college students—well, normal *genius* college students. In his conversations, he came away impressed—blown away, he'd later admit—by their overall aptitude.

Maybe I was a little premature in my assessment.

He'd been a little surprised to find out how intent the administration was to broaden the students' education beyond engineering and science. They even had a humanities requirement. Maybe it was working.

These guys did look sort of human.

•

He'd walked by the future chapter house. It was impressive—and also impressively old. It would definitely need some work. He'd been invited to participate in the meetings with the City of Cambridge Zoning Board. MIT wanted to make sure they could turn this into undergraduate housing. The plan was to demolish the upper stories in the building's rear center, which would create a nice deck, perfect for outdoor parties.

I approve.

Cambridge was one of the country's leading voices for what was then termed "handicapped access." The leading proponents from Cambridge would go on to be significant contributors to the Americans with Disabilities Act that would be passed in 1990. The renovated building was going to be accessible. No ifs, ands, or buts.

The plan involved a long "S"-shaped ramp from the back to allow wheelchair access to the first floor of the building from the rear alleyway.

Corky had been one of the ramp's most vocal proponents. Although he envisioned a somewhat different use for the gently-sloping entranceway.

That's going to be perfect for rolling kegs up into the house.

16

Risk Aversion

Al Mink had applied for the job of Residence/Orientation (R/O) chairman during the second semester of his freshman year. Not only was it a position that he thought would be fun and challenging, but it was one in which he could make a difference.

Be careful what you ask for.

Initially surprised at being selected, he quickly took to the job. In his position, he worked with Dean Bonnie Kellerman, whose corner office on the Institute's infinite corridor was passed by nearly every student every day.

Along with a few others, Al became "rent-a-student." Whenever Dean Kellerman needed a student representative for parents' day, donors' day, receptions, and other events, Al got the call. It wasn't all bad. Many times, the events were catered events with upscale food and drink, including high-caliber beer and wine.

Don't mind if I do.

In his position, Al got to know Dean of Housing Kenneth Browning and Dean for Student Affairs Carola Eisenburg. There was no question about it—Al was "connected."

Through his connections, Al had heard about the board's decision to increase enrollment and their concerns about finding sufficient undergraduate housing to accommodate the increasing numbers in the already crowded housing mix of dormitories and fraternities.

Al got wind of the fact that a new fraternity—and a women's living group—were in the mix of possible solutions. He'd heard that MIT already had a building in place in their portfolio of properties.

Al was therefore keenly aware of what the President's Annual Report of 1975-1976 stated in its section on housing:

> We are therefore exploring other alternatives to meet the predicted over-demand in September 1977 if we are to maintain a first-year class size of 1,100, which is the current target figure.
>
> We have embarked on a program to develop two independent residences—a fraternity for approximately 50 men and a cooperative for about 50 women—in an older apartment house, formerly owned by the Northgate Community Corporation, on Massachusetts Avenue, a few blocks north of the main Institute buildings.

Coincidentally, there just happened to be, at the very same time, an international fraternity that was seeking to resurrect and reconnect a local chapter.

MIT, meet ADP. ADP, meet MIT.

From the housing office's point of view, there wasn't much time left to get these new groups up and running— that is, if they wanted to have their "older apartment house" occupied—at least in part—by the Fall semester.

And it just so happened that they had a student who was working for them, one who had all the qualities you could ask for to help start a fledgling fraternity chapter. In terms of their risk aversion, this guy was the total package.

Al, meet Corky. Corky, meet Al.

They met in the Dean's office. Rather than an interview, Al

got a distinct impression that he was being recruited.

From Corky's point of view, this made perfect sense. His job was to draft a core group of pledges to start the fraternity. The student who sat across from him had already been vetted and recommended by the Dean himself.

Talk about a no-brainer.

Corky did his job well, and Al's name was entered into his ledger.

Corky was happy. Al was happy. And MIT was very happy.

Isn't it nice to be wanted?

A Cork of Fate

In late March or early April of 1976, it popped up in hallways, common areas, and entrances of MIT dormitories.

The nondescript, and relatively sparse flyer, simply stated that a new fraternity was being started at MIT, and it provided the number to call for those interested.

I was living in the newest dormitory at MIT, appropriately named "New House" until a wealthy donor gifted the Institute with a donation that exceeded some undisclosed threshold, at which time the dormitory would bear their name in perpetuity.

I note with some amusement that the dormitory today is still named New House and that an even newer dormitory was built alongside it on Memorial Drive, with the equally improbable, but similarly pleasing name of "Next House."

New House appears to have acquired at some point a reputation as the worst dormitory at MIT, although, at the time, some of the oldest dormitories, such as Bexley Hall and East Campus, had far worse physical structures, and seemed to attract the more "eccentric" students.

The dorm was divided into six individual "houses." Since the dormitory opened with my class year, the vast majority of the occupants were freshmen. In two of the houses, several floors were set aside for special purpose "cultural" houses. In "French House" and "Russian House," students lived and conversed in their second language as a quick and effective way of becoming fluent.

The top floors of Russian house became the area known affectionately by its residents as "Chocolate City." Though not officially designated at the time, Chocolate City had become a magnet housing center for many African-American students at MIT.

I was in one of the "regular" houses, i.e., one without any special designation. I was by no means dissatisfied—and one of my fellow residents had told me at one point that I was so well respected, I could have run for any house office, and easily won. That was nice to hear.

But it was often the case that the hallways and lounges of the dorm were empty, and each person was off doing their own thing. There didn't seem to exist any commitment to make any form of coherent community—at the end of the day, it was every man for himself.

•

But back to the flyer. A startup fraternity was intriguing, but any specific details were hard to come by. At this point in history, there was no internet, no cell phones, no texting, so the amount of information we had about this new fraternity was limited to the few lines on the flyer. You had to call "Corky" at the number listed.

Corky?

So, I called.

I met with Corky at some long-forgotten location, probably a common room in my dorm. He looked like he was just out of college himself, at most a few years older than I was. His most distinguishing features were his mustache and his quirky nickname.

He exuded a "party animal" vibe, and I sensed he may have been having a little trouble finding like-minded candidates at this school for geniuses. He seemed equal-parts enthusiastic and intimidated.

Animal House, the movie, wouldn't make it to the big screen for another two years. The fictional fraternity in the movie, Delta Tau Chi, was based, in part, on co-writer Chris Miller's experiences at the Dartmouth chapter of Alpha Delta Phi. It's a virtual certainty that Corky would have led off with this fact had the movie already been out.

Corky did ask me about another person he had contacted from my dorm, a fellow by the name of Uri. I knew him, or at least, I knew *of* him.

"You don't want Uri," I said. "He won the first annual 'asbestos cork' award."

Corky shot me a defensive look.

"What's the matter with corks?"

Whoops.

"Nothing wrong with corks," I backpedaled. "As a matter of fact, I like corks. Always have."

Corky seemed mollified, but still somewhat puzzled.

"It's just *this* cork," I continued. "It's the annual award for the biggest flaming asshole in the dorm. Uri won it unanimously."

Comprehension gradually replaced his earlier puzzlement. "Asbestos cork, I get it," he said, now chuckling as his mind pictured scenes of jet flames erupting from Uri's posterior.

"We certainly don't want any ass-flamers."

I watched as he crossed off the name in his ledger, destroying one student's dreams of a new life, while simultaneously preserving the dreams of the rest of us.

I was not sad.

As Mr. Spock would put it so eloquently, a few years later:

The needs of the many outweigh the needs of the few.

The Building

On a quiet night, on the top floor of the Lamson Building, a person can feel the subway approaching. Running some fifty feet underneath Main Street, and an equal distance away from the rear of the building, the low-frequency rumble from the train conducts itself along the tunnel walls, traveling through surrounding earth and soil, eventually finding its way into the building's foundation, where it seeks out natural resonance chambers.

Following the rumble, as the mass of the subway cars reaches its closest point, the entire building sways, a gentle earthquake that happens hundreds of times each day—on a regular schedule. For some, the swaying could be unnerving—if they stand perfectly still and stare out the window, they feel the oddest sensation, as if the building were about to fall over.

But logic prevailed, and they realize that this building, along with the Red Line subway, had been around for a long time, and if it were going to fall over, the odds were extremely high that it would have done so already.

At the time that we first occupied the chapter house, in 1976, that "long time" was almost seventy years. Constructed in 1907, the Lamson Building, at 351-355 Mass Ave, was one of a series of "substantial" brick structures built by Rufus Lamson, or more likely by his son, Rufus William Lamson.

The building's age and heritage combined to eventually have it designated as 'historical,' and it's located at the very corner of Central Square's historical district.

As Brother Steven Bergstein noted:

> The NPS granted the district historical status in 1990. our building lies within the National Historical Register's Central Square Historical District. (In fact, the lines appear to have been drawn specifically to include our building.)

The building appears to have been built in the great period of Cambridgeport expansion occurring at the turn of the century after the construction of the Harvard Bridge and Charles River Dam.

In 1912, only five years after the Lamson building construction, MIT moved their campus just a stone's throw away.

So, based on the historical order of events, it's technically more accurate to say that the MIT campus is conveniently located near our chapter house, rather than the other way around.

Cambridge city records show that in 1925, building alterations of $200 ($3000 today) were done by Mrs. Lamson. One wonders what sort of alterations required a city permit to accomplish.

New curtains?

The building, primarily used for apartments, had been acquired by Northgate Community Corporation, a non-profit set up by MIT to consolidate their real-estate holdings. This was not surprising, as nearly all commercial real estate in Cambridge is snapped up by either MIT or Harvard, as evidence of each University's unwavering commitment to institutional Lebensraum.

By 1976, MIT was struggling to keep up with the needs for undergraduate housing. Roughly 3000 students resided in MIT dorms, while 1000 or so lived in the so-called independent living groups, of which the thirty or so fraternities made up the bulk.

MIT relied heavily on fraternities to prevent massive

overcrowding in existing dormitory space.

But new dormitories were expensive. New House, MIT's newest dorm, and my residence during my freshman year was completed in 1975 for $25,000 per student-room, not including the land. In 2021 dollars, that's equivalent to $125,000 per student-room.

Yikes!

And at the prevailing mortgage interest rates in 1976, somewhere north of eight percent, MIT couldn't recoup their costs for the new dorm through student rental income. That wouldn't occur until a generous donor was found who could pay off a good chunk of the dorm's capital costs. As the President's annual report bluntly stated:

> Since new house construction is so expensive (currently about $25,000 per student bed over and above the land costs) and since only a small fraction of the total capital cost of new student housing can be amortized from rental income at rates prevailing at M.I.T., we are hesitant to move into additional new construction until such time as significant gift money is available.

It's no surprise that MIT was amenable to working with national fraternities to create more undergraduate living space, while hopefully saving millions of dollars in infrastructure costs.

The MIT housing department determined that the apartment property at 351-355 would be perfect for another fraternity, coupled with a new women's living group.

The cost of procuring and renovating this apartment building was projected to be far less than building a new dormitory; in fact, some sixty percent less. The president's annual report continued:

> Project cost, including purchase price but not including provisions for parking, is projected at $1 million or $10,000 per bed for 100 beds.

But first things first—they needed to kick out the existing tenants. This was not well-received by the current residents, many of whom were MIT graduate students.

Such is the price of progress.

The Next Step

Corky's recruiting efforts had resulted in a "core" group of three—myself, Al Mink, and Louis Cohen. All of us had the same experience with fraternity organization, fraternity life, and fraternity startups—i.e., none.

"What's the next step?" we asked Corky in our first group meeting. Somehow, we knew the answer, even before we asked.

We need to throw a party!

With little time to waste, plans were made for a chapter recruitment party to be held on Friday, April 23, on the grounds of MacGregor House, one of MIT's dorms.

We formulated the copy for the publicity poster and had posters printed at Gnomon copy, the local printing house of choice. In the day, we had no computers with fancy software packages. All layout and design were all done at the printing house.

Social media involved flyers and posters on cork bulletin boards.

Our poster, in every aspect, was exactly what you might

26

expect from a joint effort of three MIT students and one fraternity field rep. At the top, in bold caps, in bright red, was simply one word:

PARTY

No exclamation point. Clearly, this part of the poster was Corky's contribution to the brain trust.

The next three lines, just under PARTY, still in all-caps, centered in a blocky, modernish font, contain the poster's core message.

FOR INDIVIDUALS INTERESTED
IN THE FOUNDING OF THE
ΑΔΦ FRATERNITY

Such masterful prose could only have been produced from the combined and prolonged efforts of three genius-level IQs.

The message only makes sense when read in conjunction with PARTY. See above.

Not content with mere men, we insisted on "individuals." It's not clear what the alternative would be.

Corky was back in the game, however, dictating that the Greek letters must be the same bright red font as PARTY, which, he argued, tied all the design elements together.

The next line, bold, black, and beautiful, and still in all-caps, had text so large that the first and last letters scraped the poster sides. It used a friendlier, more approachable font.

MUSIC — BEER — MUNCHIES

This line also had Corky's fingerprints all over it. One imagines the conversation at the printing center.

"How large do you want this line to be?" they ask.

"As large as is humanly possible!"

Three of Corky's four essential party ingredients were included here.* Beer and food, "munchies," in the day, would be

---

* The fourth is left as an exercise to the reader.

essential to attract a crowd. We had no music to speak of, at least that I can recall, and in fact, loud music would have hindered communication, but Corky could not imagine a party without any music, so he led with it.

The time and place of the event, next, finally broke the all-caps theme. And at the bottom were our phone numbers, five-digit "dorm-line" numbers that, at the time, could only make calls to, or be called from, other dorms or MIT offices.

The rules for posting on all campus bulletin boards (*No Exceptions!*) were that everything posted needed an expiration date and a contact number. We qualified.

Thankfully, there were no requirements for a minimum level of stylistic competence.

I'm sure the graphic designers at Gnomon copy stared in awe as the first copy of our poster rolled out of their presses—before they burst out laughing. We certainly made their day.

Whatever its appearance, the poster was sure to attract attention, and we soon had a stack of "multicolor" 12x18 posters, printed on beige card stock, in our possession.

The three of us assessed our finalized work. I believe that we were genuinely pleased with our combined graphic design effort.

Each armed with a small stack, we then set off to make as many "posts" as possible in our allocated dormitories.

PARTY

FOR INDIVIDUALS INTERESTED IN THE FOUNDING OF THE ΑΔΦ FRATERNITY

MUSIC — BEER — MUNCHIES

9:00pm, Friday, April 23,
in the MacGregor Dining Hall

For more information call Al 5-8454
Louis 5-6239
Tony 5-7452
Corky 3-2170

The infamous poster

Who Are We Looking For, Anyway?

In our initial meetings, we discussed among ourselves how we would present the fraternity in its most promising light. Perhaps we could focus on the attractive personal qualities of our initial core group.

I looked at Louis. Louis looked at Al. Al looked at me.

"Maybe we should have a plan B," I suggested.

We nodded in silent agreement.

●

But what's the best way to go about selecting someone to be part of your fraternity "family?" Someone with whom you'd be living for up to three more years. We didn't have a handbook, or any experience, to give us any guidance.

I thought about the qualities I'd want in a biological brother, if, by some miracle, I'd had the chance to interview for mine instead of having to take the one my parents gave me.

"Someone who didn't hog the bathroom" might be high up on my list. But that was a topic we probably didn't want to broach with our potential recruits.

30

But there were at least a few attributes that stood out. First and foremost, we were looking for people who seemed as if they would be easy to get along with. A brilliant fraternity brother would be fantastic. A condescendingly brilliant one would not be.

A flaming asshole? Well, as a famous person would put it some ten years later.

Just say no!

Secondly, it would be nice if they brought something to the table—that is, besides an appetite. Were they interesting? Did they have any unique abilities or talents? Did they have a vision, or a passion, for anything? What would this person add to our frat?

Thirdly, I must admit, we wanted to filter out "dorks." It wasn't our job to judge a person's worth, but we at least wanted brothers with some degree of social aptitude.

After pondering all our desired attributes, I began to seriously wonder if *I* possessed the requisite qualities we were looking for in a brother.

I'm not worthy!

Fortunately, that period of intense self-reflection was brief, and all but forgotten in the events of the moment.

•

This party would be, in effect, our first "rush," one that took place over the span of only a few hours, and one in which all decisions would have to be made quickly and decisively. The timetable didn't allow a lot of time for deep reflection.

We wouldn't realize, until many years later, that people, in general—and in particular—do an extremely poor job at interviewing. For employment interviews, the correlation between the interviewer's impression of a candidate and their subsequent job performance is almost nil. In some ways, it was a crapshoot.

Sometimes, it pays to be ignorant.

•

Fortunately, we had some resources to pull from—Alpha Delt alumni.

David Eddy, an Alpha Delt alum from Union college, lived

in the area and had been recruited to assist with our startup efforts. Not only did he have fraternity experience, but at ten years our senior, he brought an air of maturity and respectability into our ranks.

It didn't hurt that he also had a great story. In addition to being a computer genius, an attribute that enabled him to effectively interface with your typical MIT gnurd[*], he was a character—he raced motorcycles in his spare time.

David had majored in Russian history as an undergraduate, then took one computer course in his final semester, which he parlayed into what would become a fifty-year career in the software biz.

Whenever we would begin to falter in our conversation efforts with a potential recruit, a lightbulb would go off.

"Have you met David, yet?"

Problem solved.

Corky also brought fraternity experience into the room, although his experience often presented itself more along the lines of "have another beer."

Corky confidently embodied the social side of the fraternity, which proved to be an attractive attribute for many.

After all, we were selling futures.

•

We did have a few other selling points. Our biggest was the promise of a completely renovated building by the following year.

In today's environment, we'd have a nifty CGI preview of the new digs, probably with a VR interface.

In 1976, we were limited to simply describing the wonderfulness that was to come—generally accomplished, to best effect, by staring off into the heavens with a look of great bliss.

Another attraction was the location. We'd be the first fraternity to be located on Mass Ave in Cambridge. Only a ten-minute walk to the campus, we were close to stores, restaurants, and the Central Square "T" station.

----

[*] Official MIT spelling

32

And did I mention that we're directly across the street from a pub?

•

We had the distinct feeling that our MIT overlords were monitoring our progress. They'd promised to provide us with a building in the fall—one that would have the capacity for up to sixty brothers by the start of the following year.

We were vaguely aware if we blew it now, the Institute could step in to make sure their investment would not be wasted. Such a feeling was not mere paranoia.

Indeed, in the president's annual report, he alluded to this potentiality:

> This project is unique because of the Institute ownership and control of a facility being created for independent living groups. The project operates on the premises that 1) I. R. D. F. financing will be available in the near future, and 2) the facility could be suitable for an Institute House if the independent groups do not survive.

Big brother was watching us, monitoring our progress, ready to take over and turn the building into a dorm if we screwed up.

No pressure.

•

Our story was fairly simple. We had MIT's backing for a new fraternity. We had a chapter house in place, one that would need a lot of work to make it habitable for the first year. We needed to accomplish a tremendous amount in a short period of time.

And all we could promise them, for the first year at least, might be summed up in the famous words of Churchill:

Blood, toil, tears, and sweat.

•

We gathered early in the MacGregor dining hall. Posters had been out for nearly a week. I don't recall that anyone called us at the numbers we'd listed.

Corky had helped us in acquiring the "munchies" and beer

for the party, in addition to an impressive collection of alcoholic beverages and associated mixers.

"How many people do you think will come?"

No one had a clue.

Left - College-age Mike "Corky" Corcoran   Right - David Eddy on the BMW he rode across the US and down the Pan-American Highway in 1973.

David Eddy racing his Ducati

And Then There Were Ten

Adrian Zuckerman had three roommates in his overcrowded dorm room.

Living in one of Baker house's 'quads,' he liked his dorm—in general. Like most of us, he found dorm life to be acceptable, sometimes even reaching the "good" level. But one factor was lacking—a sense of community.

Adrian had already lived an extraordinary life. His family had fled from Communist Romania when he was eight, settling in Connecticut. In a decade, Adrian had mastered the English language—although with an accent that no one could quite identify—and he had excelled academically, to the point where he had been accepted to his first choice of colleges, just a few hours away from his home.

He liked his roommates—well, two of them, at least. But from year to year, he could see the mix of people on his dorm floor would be changing, and while some of the people he got to know would remain, what was missing was a core of close-knit people who had something in common besides residing on the same dormitory floor.

He had seen our poster and brought it up to Steve Ofsthun and Russ Kalis, two out of the three freshmen with whom he shared his room.

Together, they agreed that they needed to "check this thing out."

•

We noticed the group enter the dining hall, shortly after nine. I'd like to recall that we were nonchalant, cool, and collected. But more likely, we simply pounced on the unsuspecting trio. In one brief moment, we were suddenly entertaining the possibility of doubling our group's size.

This shit just got real!

Russ, Steve, and Adrian had no idea of what to expect from this party—other than music, beer, and munchies, of course. The poster had provided no information about the fraternity, other than the Greek letters. When they entered, they saw only a few people—us.

I recognized Adrian. I'd played with him on the freshman squash team. We'd both learned how to play squash after joining the team, as did most of its freshmen members. And we'd already shared the "brotherhood of the squash welt," that peculiar, donut-shaped bruise you receive after your opponent drills the rock-hard rubber squash ball directly into your back or butt.

"Sorry."

The group of three roommates was divided and the process of round-robin interviews began. It wouldn't end until all attendees had parted for the evening.

But first, as always, we had to give them our top-secret fraternity greeting.

"Want a beer?"

Steve was cheery, affable, and seemed like he would make the perfect fraternity brother. Personable, athletic, and smart, of course, it was immediately apparent, even after talking with him for only a few minutes, that he would be easy to get along with.

I think I'm going to like this guy.

36

There is a word that perfectly describes a certain type of person.

Stolid.

Unfortunately, at that time, I didn't know that word.

But I knew exactly what it represented.

Russ Kalis was stolid.

Calm, dependable, a man of few words, you could tell Russ was the kind of guy who would just "get things done," with little fanfare or drama.

And we were going to need a lot of things done if we were going to be up and running by September.

Adrian was personable, funny, and confident. It was clear that he wasn't desperate to join our merry band, and that he was checking us out—perhaps even more than the opposite.

Wait a minute. We're the ones doing the interviewing.

Each person got a chance to talk with Corky and David, who were able to give them a much better picture of fraternity life than our mere guesses could.

•

Jon Cohen had seen Corky's initial flyer and had some interest but hadn't pursued it.

He'd been interested in fraternities in his first R/O week rush but wasn't offered a bid. He had heard that Baker House, had a reputation of being somewhat more like a frat than most dorms.

And it had been okay, except when he found out who his roommate would be the following year. That had the potential of being problematic. It was time for a change.

When he saw the poster for the party, just a short walk from his dorm, via Amherst Alley, he followed up on his initial interest by heading over to the party—fashionably late, of course.

Analytical and detail-oriented, Jon questioned us about the specifics of the fraternity. All we could tell him was what we knew at the time, which was short on details, and heavy on vision and promise.

•

When I saw Rob "Moose" Mandel enter our collective, I was thrilled. Another freshman squash teammate! This made things decidedly easier.

I had already known that Rob was funny, perceptive, and insightful. He was not hesitant to ask probing questions but didn't turn into an arrogant jerk when we weren't able to provide him with all the details. He just nodded his head, appearing to "take things under consideration."

Rob recalls having a serious conversation with Al and myself. I recollect that we tried hard not to "sell" him, or anyone, for that matter, on the fraternity. We wanted everyone to know that it would be a lot of work in the short term to get everything going.

If you weren't up for that, maybe this wasn't for you. But, if you were, in a year, you'd end up in one of the nicest houses on campus.

Did I ask you how you feel about deferred gratification?

I recalled a conversation I'd had with Rob in the weight room of the gym a few months earlier. Rob was trying to convince me to start doing some weight training. I was all of 135 pounds at the time, and at 5'-10", could have used a little more muscle on my frame.

I told him I'd tried it for a while, but nothing seemed to be happening.

He told me that I didn't "weight" long enough.

I liked Rob.

•

When Bob Anderson walked in, the spirit in the room immediately improved. Bob, perhaps the only true extrovert in our midst, greeted everyone with a smile and a compliment—and that was his nature. He wasn't being smarmy.

It was almost impossible not to like Bob. Friendly, cheerful, always willing to help out, you always felt better after a conversation with him.

We didn't interview Bob. We simply discussed our plans for the fraternity, and he told us how great our vision seemed to be, and added a few ideas of his own.

I don't think we ever seriously entertained not offering him a bid.

•

When Bob Wolf entered and told us his name, we began to wonder what was making this chapter so attractive to all the Roberts of the world.

Bob Wolf was the only MIT undergraduate present who had any fraternity experience.

He was living in one.

As a boarder.

As a sophomore, Bob had transferred to MIT after his freshman year at another institution. Coming from the nearby town of Newton, he'd lived at home his first semester.

After a semester of commuting, he felt like he was missing out on a big part of the college experience. When he heard about an opening for a boarder at the Delta Kappa Epsilon frat (Deke), he'd jumped at the chance.

Then, upon seeing the poster for our party, just two buildings away at MacGregor, he jumped even higher.

He recalls asking Louis what kinds of people we were looking for.

"We're just looking for nice guys," came the reply.

That sounded like a surprisingly good fit.

•

It was non-stop intensive conversation from the moment the first group entered until the last one said goodnight. And then we had to meet and confer to make our decisions.

David Eddy recalls that, before the party, he didn't know what to expect from a group of MIT freshmen. Much like Corky, before meeting us, or with our potential pledges, he wondered if a group of MIT freshmen had what it took to start a new chapter of his beloved frat. After all, he'd heard the stories about MIT people.

However, after that night, he was encouraged enough to contact fellow Union alum Paul Stewart to join the effort.

"I think these guys are going to be alright."

At the end of the day—or evening, in this case—we'd made offers to at least eight potential pledges. Within a day or so, seven had accepted our invitation.

•

What did these seven have in common—apart from attending MIT and having serious smarts? Not much, besides a professed willingness to put in the work that was going to be necessary. Only one, Bob Anderson, could be considered outgoing.

Adrian was a born leader. Steve, athletic and helpful. Russ, super competent and capable.

Bob Wolf was our optimist, Jon Cohen, our detail-oriented management guru, and Rob (Moose) Mandel was amazingly insightful and hilariously funny.

Every single person we pledged brought a different skill set to the table. And we'd need to utilize every one of them to if we wanted to turn a vision into a reality.

We hadn't "taken off" yet, but the wheels were definitely beginning to leave the runway.

•

For some reason, the pledge training materials handed out in 1983 have a slightly different version of the events of this timeframe. According to this "alternate history":

> Twelve additional men were found who were willing to commit themselves to the new group. Three of these would lose interest over the next month. Also, two of the Seniors in the group dropped out when it became clear that the residence they would occupy for their final year at MIT would be an old apartment building undergoing renovations. Those that remained became the "Original Ten:"

Trying to decipher this text is difficult. It seems to indicate that we issued bids to twelve people at the party, five of whom dropped out or lost interest for various reasons, leaving us with seven, who, when combined with Al, Louis, and myself, became the "Original Ten™."

I believe this account is a little suspect since any Seniors would have known at the time they committed that the frat's first year would be in the old building. This account may be conflating some earlier startup attempts about which I'm not familiar.

●

We did have quite a supply of liquor leftover from our party. Since I would be staying over the summer in my dorm, I volunteered to hold on to our supply for safekeeping. For some reason, the supply dwindled significantly over the summer months.

Must have been the cockroaches.

A Dream Realized

"Henry," the voice on the phone began, in an earnest and important tone. "It's Burt Price, I've got some good news."

It took Henry Leeb a few seconds to associate the voice with the name and to bring these together into his cognition.

"Oh yes, Burt. How are you."

Burton Price had met Henry through Burt's son Scott. They had subsequently become great friends. Burt, an Alpha Delta alum from Hamilton College in 1923, was the guiding influence of the Alpha Delta Phi Foundation, and a founding member of the Corporation.

Through his friendship with Henry, he'd learned of the latter's long, and to date, futile attempts to join his Lambda Phi chapter with the International Alpha Delta Phi fraternity.

Burt jumped right into the purpose of his call.

"Wesleyan University has agreed to make you an honorary member of the faculty."

Henry recalled that Burt was an alumnus of Wesleyan University and a generous donor. It was clear he'd pulled some strings.

42

"That's nice," Henry responded. "That's an honor."

"This means you're eligible."

"Eligible? For what? To teach a class? Did you forget I'm eighty-two? What am I going to teach, advanced geriatrics?"

"As an honorary faculty member," Burt explained, "you'll be eligible to be initiated into Alpha Delta Phi at the Middletown chapter. They've agreed. It's going to happen on April 3."

Henry had to sit down for a moment to take it all in. His plans had been dormant for so long that it took a while to realize that what he had long hoped for—or at least part of it—was going to take place.

"And that's not everything," Burt continued, "we're starting an Alpha Delta Phi chapter at MIT."

This was the other task that Henry had been working on for so long. But there had been so many disappointments in the past.

"Is it real this time?" Henry questioned. "Remember back in, when was it... sixty-one?"

"We've met with the administration. They're desperate for more space for undergraduate housing. They've got a building. They've given us the go-ahead. We're sending our field rep to get a core group going. It's going to happen."

Henry pondered this news. He wasn't altogether certain that he'd still be around by the time this whole process was completed. But he had some ideas about starting a new chapter. He began to write a letter in his head, with instructions about what needed to be done.

And as he did, a small smile started to creep across his face.

•

The initiation ceremony was held, as planned, on April 3 at the Middletown chapter in Middletown, Connecticut, just south of Hartford. Henry received his badge from his granddaughter's husband, Thomas Neely, Kenyon '74.

Three weeks later, he received another call, this time from Bob McKelvey.

"Corky's done a great job at MIT. They've got a core group of students who've committed to start the chapter."

This was enough for Henry to start putting down his thoughts on paper. He wrote a long letter to Bob with instructions for starting up the new chapter. He began to plan a trip to Cambridge from his current residence in Somerset, NJ.

Perhaps it was the excitement of the news. Perhaps the fulfillment of what he had dreamed about for so long was sufficient enough. Perhaps... it was simply his time. A sudden streptococcus infection proved to be too much for him. Henry Leeb passed away the next day, in many ways, fulfilled.

Rest in peace, Brother Leeb.

Getting Organized

With our "gang of ten" firmly established, we began to formulate plans for the summer and fall.

First item – selection of officers.

Al was the obvious candidate for our first President. He already had the MIT connections, which we would need to utilize if, and when, any issues arose.

But Al already had major commitments, including Air Force ROTC, and had a desire to graduate in three years, and felt that he couldn't undertake the responsibility. He did agree to serve as vice-president and to provide help and assistance to the president.

Adrian stepped up as the first president. An eternal optimist. Adrian exuded confidence that we would succeed. Not only did he profess it, he also genuinely believed that it would happen.

It didn't take long to find our second office-holder. I had experience running the cooking group in my freshman dorm. There was no opposition to me serving as the first food steward, a position I'd soon find out had time-consuming and seemingly neverending, responsibilities.

Similarly, the other major time-intensive house office, that of treasurer, couldn't simply be appointed. Someone would have to agree to take on the responsibility. Jon Cohen was willing and able.

Russ Kalis took on the role of house manager. His temperament and take-charge attitude were a perfect fit for making sure things got done.

Rob Mandel took on the job of athletics and would oversee our involvement in intramural athletics.

Louis agreed to be the first house critic, a perfect choice for his acerbic wit.

Steve took on the duties of house secretary, which meant that he was the one to take notes of the meeting we were having at this very moment.

Get out your pen, Steve!

Bob Wolf was our first pledge trainer, which was unique in that none of us had even pledged at this point. Bob had to assemble some of the ADP history and lore that we would be required to learn prior to our own initiation. Afterward, he'd focus on our new pledge class.

Bob Anderson was our first social chairman, a role that fitted him perfectly. Bob had great connections with Wellesley College and immediately began formulating plans for social events for the fall. Planning the fraternity's social calendar was right in Bob's wheelhouse.

We had no historian, which, in hindsight, was an overwhelming omission. As a result, few pictures and details of our early history were captured, and records of many such events exist only in the fading memories of the few brothers who were present.

I'd use my time in the Spring to contact the IFC. They were more than happy to provide me the list of food vendors used by the frats, along with instructions. We'd need to get geared up to hit the ground running (eating?) for our upcoming work week at the end of the summer.

Tony Pelham

ADRIAN ZUCKERMAN
PRESIDENT 1ST. TERM

ALLAN MINK
VICE PRESIDENT

47

STEPHEN OFSTHUN
SECRETARY 1ST. TERM

RUSSELL KALIS
HOUSE MANAGER

ANTHONY PELHAM
FOOD STEWARD

JONATHAN COHEN
TREASURER

ROBERT MANDEL
ATHLETIC CHAIR.

ROBERT WOLF
PLEDGE TRAINER IST. TERM

LOUIS COHEN
CRITIC IST. TERM

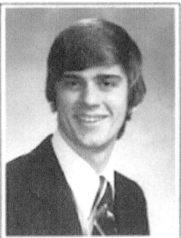

ROBERT ANDERSON
SOCIAL CHAIR. IST .TERM

•

Immediately after the party, the ten of us were "committed."
But not in a bad way.

It's just that we had no official status in the fraternity other
than being committed to join. That changed on May 21st, as the
Board formally pledged the ten of us. A copy of the letter sent to

Robert Price from the "Lamda" Phi Fraternity, signed by nine of the ten, requested formal acceptance into Alpha Delta Phi.

We're MIT students. We never said we could spell.

LAMDA PHI FRATERNITY
351 Massachusetts Avenue
Cambridge, Mass.

Mr. Robert S. Price
The Alpha Delta Phi
1600 Western Savings Bank Bldg.
Philadelphia, Pennsylvania 19107

Dear Mr. Price:

We, the undersigned students at the Massachusetts Institute of Technology, formally request The Alpha Delta Phi to accept our Society as the Lamda Phi Chapter of The Alpha Delta Phi. More than sixty years have elapsed since Lamda Phi first requested this affiliation with The Alpha Delta Phi. The passing years have proven our fidelity and devotion to our mutual purposes. We, on our part, pledge to exercise our best efforts to promote those purposes, so that we may be deemed worthy of receiving the Charter of the Lamda Phi Chapter of The Alpha Delta Phi.

Done this Friday, twenty-first day of May, 1976.

x Jonathan Cohen
x Stephen P. Ofsthun
x Adrian Zuckerman
x Robert Mandel
x Robert S. Wolf
x Louis Cohen
x Anthony J. Pelham
x ALLAN L. MINK II
x Russell Kalis

Bob Wolf recalls that we had periodic meetings with Ken Browning in the ensuing months. During one of the meetings, Ken explained how the IRDF worked. I must have missed that meeting because I still don't understand it.

It's clear that MIT housing wanted to keep tabs on our progress, and that they must have been satisfied. It's somewhat odd that they would not address issues related to providing furniture for our house, or providing us with a loan for rush expenses, both of which, as we would come to find out later, would cause us some extra headaches.

None of us wanted "Big Brother" to be watching over us at every step, but I don't think we would have minded having a "Sugar Daddy," at least for a little while during the beginning.

•

Al, Jon, and Bob Wolf took the lead in getting our summer mailings out to prospective freshmen. We had already missed the deadline for MIT-funded assistance for a summer mass mailing to incoming freshmen and transfers.

Thanks again, Dean Browning.

But, not to worry. Al procured a hardcopy listing of all the incoming students mailing addresses—data that was available to all the frats. He also had access to MIT's Multics[8] computer system.

Al had managed to codger up a rudimentary mail-merge system to generate semi-personalized letters to each freshman. All we needed to do was retype in all the names and addresses from the listing into a file, push enter, and viola[*]!

Bob Wolf remembers working to 11 pm or midnight, for many nights, typing in addresses. Al told him that to save time, he could just type in "St" for "Street," and his program would do a global substitution.

Apparently, several of our mailings ended up going to addresses in Street Louis, Missouri.

As it would turn out, this innocuous summer mailing would

---

[8] https://web.mit.edu/multics-history/
[*] Intentionally spelled incorrectly.

turn out to be one of the keys for our first rush week, now only a little over two months away.

The clock was ticking.

•

Thanks to Brother Andy Bronstein, one copy of the original summer mailing still exists and is reproduced below.

According to the letter, penned by Al Mink, the fraternity had its start in January. That seems like a bit of a stretch but may refer to some of the early organization efforts by the International, and/or Corky.

Al, as R/O week chairman, was very charitable towards other living groups, but he also wasted no time launching into reasons why we could very well be far superior to any other choice.

Distilled to its core, our pitch was that we were new, and thus new members would shape the chapter's future, we were small, we had a great location, and we had a great national organization.

At this point, he indicates that we seem to be looking for a pledge class of only ten, which makes sense, as the Institute had told us that our share of the house would hold around twenty.

He alludes to the fact that we could be moving into the renovated building in the Spring. It's conceivable at this point that the Institute had told us that this was a possibility, but logistically, it doesn't seem like there's any way that could have been achieved.

Some of our rush events had already been planned at this point. A beer tasting contest, and an unforgettable seafood dinner (prepared by a native!) where you could get SCROD at ADP.

Al alludes to the fact that freshmen could visit us on Thursday, a full day before other frats, a significant advantage.

And lastly, we promised transportation when they arrive. Not a bad deal!

July 23, 1976

Hi Andrew,

Welcome to MIT! My name is Al Mink. I'm one of ten MIT men working to make Alpha Delta Phi one of the best MIT fraternities as well as one of one of the newest. We started last January so that we would be ready for your class this fall.

Deciding upon a living group is a difficult task. Each of the dorms and the other frats has a lot of unique advantages. I think that ADP has several merits that the others don't.

1. We are new enough that you will have tremendous input in shaping ADP's future. We are still working with the architects on proposals to renovate our new house.(Some of us are already in the process of moving in.)

2. We are not out to pledge the entire freshmen class. Because renovation will force us(till spring) to live in half of the space available, we plan to pledge only 10 freshmen.

3. We have a really great location(refer to the residence handbook). Our house is off campus yet very close to the main MIT buildings. This makes a big difference when the pressures of finals are at hand and you want to get away from the 'Tute or when its -50 chill factor and the prospect of a walk across the Harvard Bridge doesn't excite you. In addition the facilities for mass transit are close by.

4. Our chapter is part of a national that has been giving us tremedous support ever since we started. We have chapters all over the nation, with a rich alumni background now living in the Boston area.

I hope that these are reasons enough, Andrew, for you to visit us during R/O week. We especially welcome you either(or both!) Friday or Saturday at the start of R/O. Friday, after the picnic, look for our signs so that we can transport you to MIT's only beer tasting contest. Can you really taste the difference? Which is best, Michelob?, Heineken?, or Coors?(we have them all) We also have an evening's worth of entertainment planned, whether you are a beer drinker or not. On Saturday night, come and get SCROD at ADP. Yes, we are cooking a dinner you will never forget, featuring Boston seafood prepared by a native of this area.

Take this as your personal invitation to partake in our rush activities this fall. If you would like more information, please write me at the address below. Also, I would be glad to give you a lift from the airport, train station, or bus station if you let me know in advance. I hope that you can stay over with us. You are invited anytime from Thursday(2nd) morning on.

Hope to hear from ya soon.

Sincerely,

Al Mink

The Budlong and the Short of It

At some point, the ten of us were provided with the names of some of the still-living Lambda Phi alumni who resided in the area, and we were urged to visit them and attempt to bring them aboard as part of the effort.

On a chilly Spring evening, several of us walked across the Harvard bridge to visit the Back Bay address that we had been provided.

Mortimer Budlong, Lambda Phi '28, then in his seventies, answered the door.

"Who's there?" he called out, gruffly.

We explained our purpose. We were going to be starting up the Lambda Phi chapter of Alpha Delta Phi, at MIT.

"Like I told the other guy, I don't want anything to do with your group. And none of the other alumni do either."

As I recall, we were more than a little taken aback. We had expected to be greeted as heroes. Instead, we found ourselves being given the bum's rush in Boston's Back Bay.

Our attempts at further explanation did nothing to dissuade him from his established position. The swift closure of his brownstone door promptly ended our conversation.

A long, cold, walk back to our dorms followed, in which it was decided that perhaps, we should table the efforts to get the older Lambda Phis on board until somebody determined exactly whose side they were on.

●

It turns out that Mortimer's assessment of the attitude of other surviving Lambda Phi alumni had been mistaken. They were not universally opposed to our efforts, and many offered their support.

The biggest surprise came, however, from Mortimer himself. He completely changed his stance. All the old Lambda Phis, including Mortimer, were inducted into Alpha Delta Phi, some posthumously. Mortimer, along with eight other Lambda Phis, would attend the initiation of our second pledge class in February.

I recall that he apologized to us for the chilly reception we received at our first meeting.

Apology accepted.

It's all good.

These "old guys" were alright, after all.

Mortimer went on to become one of the founders of the "Friends of the Lambda Phi Chapter of the Alpha Delta Phi Fraternity" Corporation, established in June 1978. He passed away a year later in Oct 1979.

It was great to have you on our side.

Workweek Cometh Before the Fall

MIT had dropped our living facility into our lap. They bought the building, worked out a deal for long-term financing, kicked out the existing tenants, and handed over the keys.

"Good luck," they said, smiling, as they drove away.

Only one small problem—there was (almost) nothing inside. No furniture, no dining room tables or chairs. No dining room. No dishes, silverware, or glasses. There was nothing to cook with.

Good luck, my ass.

In reality, they didn't even hand us the keys, we had to go pick them up. When Jon arrived at the frat house to begin work, he saw a note taped to the door:

Jon:

Please pick up the keys at the housing office.

Thanks, Al

Fraternities typically have a workweek at the end of the summer. All brothers are encouraged (incentivized? mandated?)

to come back a week before rush week. During work week various repairs, cleaning, painting, and maintenance, or upgrade projects are done to improve conditions for the coming year (or, perhaps more accurately, to repair the damage done the previous year.)

In our case, we needed every hand we could get. The building was not habitable. The building's former tenants, who were rightly miffed at being displaced from their apartments, had no incentive to leave the place in good shape for the next group. And they hadn't.

And for those who were staying on campus for the summer, the workweek was more like a "work month."

•

It isn't entirely clear where we got our initial funds. The ADP alumni group likely contributed to our startup effort. Bob McKelvey recalls that Alpha Delt alumni startup group, or the Corporation, at some point, contributed $5,000 to seed our effort.

Jon Cohen also postulates that many of the early members may have kicked in various amounts of money to kickstart the efforts, later credited to our annual dues.

•

I was on campus that summer, working in an office in the Triangle building.* I stayed in my New House dorm. Staying over the entire summer provided the opportunity to do some advance planning. Al Mink and Bob Wolf also stayed on campus.

We identified the first-floor kitchen that we would be using for meal preparation. It was a regular, apartment-sized, kitchen, which meant that cooking for the twenty-odd people that we anticipated living here for the next year would present some interesting challenges.

One of the first tasks was to get enough kitchen and dining supplies that would allow us to prepare meals in large quantities. In the pre-internet days, this meant traveling in person to downtown Boston to one of the commercial supply stores that specialized in institutional cookware and dining supplies.

---

* But that's another story.

Hopefully, they delivered.

Jon Cohen and I went down together. He had the checkbook. We managed to acquire an initial set of large pots, pans, baking sheets, dishes, glasses, silverware, and serving utensils—at least the bare minimum of what I anticipated we'd need to start preparing meals for twenty, or even more during rush week.

•

We needed more refrigerator space than the single refrigerator in the kitchen. Fortunately, a back hallway linked our kitchen to an adjacent, unused, kitchen. And the one thing that *had* been left behind in the building were the refrigerators from the building's kitchens.

Jon Cohen recalls that disgruntled ex-tenants did not feel the need to clean out their refrigerators before they were booted out. Almost all were teeming with cockroaches, one thing that MIT had bequeathed us in abundance.

Jon's first work week jobs involved pest extermination, cleaning, and moving all refrigerators downstairs into our main kitchen, or into the adjacent, auxiliary kitchen.

These extra refrigerators provided us with the cold storage we desperately needed.

•

Furniture was our next most pressing need. We had essentially no budget for furniture, and we needed to supply twenty-some rooms worth of desks and chairs, along with furniture for the common areas, and tables and chairs for the dining rooms. Pre-internet, searching and finding this kind of stuff was not so simple.

Adrian and Jon found a source for previously-owned sofas and common room furniture at Putnam's, a local furniture outlet. The stuff wasn't top quality, and we managed to destroy much of it in a short time after introducing it to fraternity life. After we got done with it, it might have been labeled as 'post-owned,' i.e., trashed.

Steve Ofsthun rests in a pre-owned chair before renovation

•

At some point, Al Mink, through his ROTC connections, clued us in on Army surplus desks and chairs that were available for only one dollar each. The only caveat—we had to go get it and transport it ourselves.

So, we rented a truck.

Jon Cohen, myself, and perhaps one other person, fit ourselves into the truck's seats and headed out to what I recall was an Army base or something similar.

I recall a vast warehouse, along the lines of "Raiders of the Lost Ark", filled from top-to-bottom with what appeared to be the heaviest furniture ever manufactured. Our goal was simple— somehow fit twenty-odd sets of desks and chairs into the back of the truck.

And they were odd.

To say the least, the furniture was not in the greatest shape. It looked like it had survived one, or possibly two, atomic blasts. But it appeared to be functional for the most part. We picked out the best pieces and over the next several hours, loaded them into the truck using what we determined was the optimal vector-packing algorithm for irregular objects in multiple dimensions.[*]

"Phew," I said, climbing back into the truck for the journey back, totally exhausted, "I'm glad that's over with."

"Umm," was the only reply.

"Umm, what?"

"Umm, this truck has to be back tomorrow morning. We've got to unload it tonight."

Shoot me now.

We pulled away from the facility, but I had a nagging feeling that something wasn't right.

Stopping to investigate, we discovered that we had neglected to pull down the rear door on the truck.

Whoops!

On the drive back, loud sounds were heard emanating from the truck's cargo area. We surmised that the entropy of our contents was increasing rapidly with every bump in the road. We hoped to make it back before the heat death of the universe.

We arrived back at the fraternity well into the evening, mercifully managing to get a parking space in front. Opening the

---

[*] Gnurd alert!

door, we saw what could only be described as the Gordian knot of Steelcase furniture.

A few other brothers met us at the house.

"Nice packing job," one proclaimed as he surveyed our work.

All I can say was that it was extremely fortunate that I was not carrying any weapons.

We collaborated for a time as to the best approach to getting the furniture up into the rooms. We all agreed that the appropriate first step would be to prop the front door open.

With the toughest decision out of the way, we then made our next bold choice.

We would use a bucket brigade!

If we lined up the brothers, we could pass furniture from one person to the next, and we could avoid having to carry the lead-lined furniture from hell.

Brilliant!

We started unloading and passing the furniture. Everything went according to plan. Only then did we notice the fundamental problem—our brigade didn't even reach the front door. Apparently, you need more than four or five people to successfully execute the bucket algorithm up three floors into a building.

Some computer nerd in the group posited that we could implement a bucket-brigade linked-list solution, where we unloaded the furniture from the first bucket-brigade to the first staging area, then reassemble our team to form a second brigade to move the furniture to the next staging area.

After a few minutes of Keystone Cops/Laurel and Hardy hijinks, we resigned ourselves to the fact that we would have to fall back to a brute-force approach.

Shoot me again.

Chairs could be carried up by one person. Desks required two people. We did make one wise decision. We loaded the upper floors first, so at least psychologically, the task would appear to get easier and faster as we went on.

That didn't fool me.

That was perhaps the most physically exhausted I can ever recall being. But, at the end of the day (night), we had desks in all the necessary places.

•

Someone came up with the brilliant idea of repurposing all the doors from the old apartment entrances into dining room tables. All we had to do was add legs, which we fashioned from 2x4 lumber. Only one problem—since Al did the "legwork" for the tables, they were sized to his impressive height. For nearly everyone else, the tables came up to shoulder level.*

Rob Mandel recalls being on a work team that stripped the paint from the entryway walls, exposing the beautiful dark wood underneath, and wondering why anyone would want to paint over such a thing?

As Rob likes to point out, he spent his first week at the fraternity working as a "stripper."

No one currently around seems to recall how we acquired our beds and mattresses. Perhaps the Institute provided them from their warehouse of such things.

After all, if they weren't going to be used for us, they would be required for the dormitories to meet all the Institute's 'overcrowding' needs.

---

* All the alumni I've talked to commented on the high table heights. No one seems to recall why we didn't take an hour or so at some point to cut a few inches off the legs.

Institutional Meltdown

"At the present time, overcrowding is economically more feasible than building additional dormitories." [9]

MIT appeared to be content with some degree of "overcrowding" in its dormitory system. MIT's decision to increase each year's undergraduate class size from 1000 to 1100 meant, eventually, there would be 400 more students who needed housing.

ADP and the Women's Independent Living Group (WILG) were a part of this solution.

Increasing the class size to 1100 doesn't seem like it would be "rocket science"—well, maybe it was rocket science at a place like MIT—but several factors made it difficult for the administration to hit the bullseye.

Each year, MIT offers admissions to a target number of students. The actual number who accept, termed the "yield," determines, to a large extent, the size of the incoming class.

---

[9] Ken Browning in The Tech Sep 17, 1976, v95-29.

But during the summer, a certain number of freshmen who had accepted admission change their minds. This is known as the "melt."

MIT can tweak a low yield by offering additional admissions from the waiting list. And they can account for the melt by offering admission to a higher-than-desired number, and hoping the melt brings it down, in a similar fashion to the airlines booking strategies.

Only in the case of MIT, extra students don't get "bumped." A portion of them just end up in overcrowded dorm rooms.

The chart below shows the "acceptance rate" curve, in gold, along with the total number of applicants, in blue, over a roughly forty-year period. In the '70s the acceptance rate ran around one-third. As applications have skyrocketed, with a mostly fixed class size, the acceptance rate has plummeted to less than seven percent in recent years.

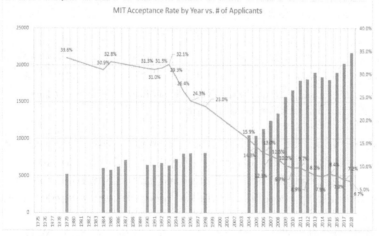

MIT Acceptance Rate by Year vs. # of Applicants

Of course, acceptance rates are different for men, women, international students, and various other groups, reflecting MIT's desired student mix.

The class of '78 numbered 1025. The class of '79 (my class), admitted in 1975, came in at 1155, at the time, the largest class ever admitted. This class was the first of several large classes intended to boost the number of undergraduates to between 4400 to 4500. [10]

The opening of the New House dorm (my freshman dorm) in 1975, which housed 350 residents, had helped to swallow up the record number of freshmen and had reduced dormitory overcrowding in general. But the construction of the dorm had been extremely costly, and no new dorm construction was on the immediate horizon.

And the class of '80 was targeted at 1100 freshmen.

Of course, the number of freshmen is not the only factor in dormitory overcrowding. Fraternities (and other independent living groups) housed about a third of the undergraduates. But the number of freshmen who pledge a fraternity depends on many factors, most of which cannot be accounted for by the MIT housing office.

Each frat had its own "yield" and "melt" numbers. Frats can't easily accommodate much overcrowding, but they can tolerate a certain number of empty rooms, since many of their costs, like food and utilities, scale with the number of residents. A frat handing out too many bids may end up in trouble. Falling short by a small number may be preferable.

But another factor comes into play. The number of freshman slots in each frat varies from year to year, depending on the number of seniors who graduate, or others who leave for various reasons. Consolidated over all the frats, the number of openings for new students across all frats is not a constant from year to year.

It doesn't appear that the MIT housing office incentivized fraternities, in any manner, to hit higher target numbers to help alleviate dorm overcrowding. I don't recall any pressure from MIT regarding our chapter's initial rush targets.

ADP and WILG, in their first year of operation, were slotted together to handle roughly forty freshmen, which was essentially all that the current facility had room for. We had a strong incentive to fill the house, not only for financial reasons but also to keep each pledge class at more or less the same size, which would be desirable in the years to come.

It wouldn't be until the end of rush week that we'd find out

---

[10] The Tech Sep 4, 1975, v95-29.

how well we'd done.

Under Achievement

Our chapter house's basement was enormous. As in "Tesla Gigafactory" enormous. Comprising an entire additional floor, the building's basement was partitioned into just a few rooms and vast expanses of empty space. It was huge and promising, in addition to being dark, dusty, dank, and ominous.

The basement, by way of the building's center entrance at 353 Mass Ave, had housed at least one commercial establishment—a barbershop. Al Mink recalls that the barbershop operated for a few months while we were occupying the building.

This likely occurred in the summer months before we officially occupied the building, until the time the barbershop was relocated elsewhere in Cambridge, most likely with MIT's assistance. The barbershop had one additional feature—a squatter—termed the "urchin." An urchin was MIT-speak for a thief, uninvited visitor, or other similarly undesirable Cambridge resident. The name seems sure to have derived from Dickensian lore.

The urchin had taken up residence in a supply closet in the basement barbershop. Russ Kalis recalls that he resided there for most of our first year. At some point, we boarded up, or otherwise blocked off, access from the barbershop to the rest of the basement, so that the lone resident could not wander into our living quarters.

This also blocked off access to any functional bathrooms, so he simply began using a corner of the barbershop to make his daily "deposits."

It's not clear how we finally convinced the last remaining apartment resident to move out, but most likely it involved the efforts of either the campus police or their Cambridge counterparts. The cleanup crew for the area during the next year's workweek was most unhappy.

This was not the type of barbershop stool they had expected to find.

The urchin later became known as the "hermit" in fraternity lore, and his former barbershop quarters are referred to as the "Hermit's Room."

•

Another basement room contained upwards of twenty phones. We puzzled over the meaning of this incongruity. The consensus was that this room may have been the location of an "under the radar" bookmaking operation.

At the time, owning your phone was not allowed. All phones had to be rented from "Ma Bell." It's hard to believe that they had no idea of what was going on there. It's also unknown whether they eventually came by and reclaimed their goods.

•

Coin-operated washers and dryers, a gift from Alpha Delta alumni, were installed into the basement's open space, quickly resolving one of the issues on our to-do list. Brother Rob Mandel was in charge of collecting the machines' coinage—25¢ for a wash, and 10¢ for a "good" dry. WILG used our machines also, apparently without our specific consent.

Brother Mandel "coined" the term for his collection organization—the "AFL-CIO,"—which stood for the "**A**lpha

Delt **F**und for **L**aundering, **C**leaning, and **I**mmaculatory* **O**perations."

Rob claims that being head of the Cambridge chapter of the AFL-CIO was extremely helpful to his resume. In a short time, his underground money-laundering scheme made him the richest person in the frat, and soon brought in enough money to buy additional washers and dryers, teaching him a valuable economics lesson:

Purchase of basement laundry equipment is a "sunk" cost.

●

Our initial reconnoiter of the building's bowels identified the perfect candidate for a dining room, now the site of the pub, just off the main stairwell.

●

A group of Alpha Delta alums from other chapters prepared the interior of the CR, as all twenty-two of us were still pledges and therefore not allowed to enter.

Ventilation was so poor, that, when occupied by more than a handful of people, the term "stuffy" proved wholly inadequate.

●

At some point, we acquired a ping-pong table, which we located in the space just off the main stairwell. For the more competitive players, I set up a wall-mounted challenge ladder holding each player's name on a round key-tag. As I recall, I was by far the best player and the reigning champion.

Writing the chapter's history does have its advantages.

●

And that was all for our first year. Vast empty basement rooms sat dormant, ripe for exploitation and colonization by future pledge classes for their work-week projects. I don't believe any of us envisioned, at the time, that this underground labyrinth would someday house a movie room, a hot tub, and a music room.

---

* Not a real word.

It's not that we wouldn't have approved of such things if we had conceived of them. It's just that we simply didn't have the time or funds to undertake any major basement upgrades.

Certainly, none of us felt that such efforts were "beneath" us.

Rush/Overview

Our own Al Mink, as R/O Week Chairman, penned an article in the Tech during the summer. He offered his take on freshmen goals:

> The two goals of R/O are:
>
> 1. To help you select your living group and your classes, and
>
> 2. To have one of the best times of your life. [11]

He went on to say that R/O Week was divided into two components.

---

[11] v96-27 The Tech July 30, 1976

All of this preparation is made to help you with two decisions about the fall term; where to live and what courses to take. R/O week is broken down physically into two parts, with emphasis from Friday ([Sep] 3) through Monday ([Sep] 6) placed upon residence selection.
12

At MIT, up until 2002, freshmen were allowed to join and reside in fraternities starting from their very first week. From the moment they set foot on campus, in only three days, nearly 400 freshmen, a third of the freshman class, would end up joining one of MIT's thirty fraternities, or other independent living groups, and the remaining two-thirds would decide in which dormitory to reside.

The process of determining who went where was anything but simple. There were significant logistical issues. During R/O Week, over 1000 students had to be housed each night, either in the dorms or fraternities. Somebody had to keep track of available beds so that each student had a place to sleep each night.

Somebody had to know where each student was, at all times, so that they could be contacted. Also, somebody had to arrange transportation to shuttle students to and from far-off frats when needed.

That "somebody" was the R/O center, the centralized operations center that kept track of each freshman's location at all times. The R/O center had contact numbers for each fraternity's rush desk, in addition to all the dormitories.

In the pre-internet, pre-smartphone, pre-computer era, keeping track of students was done using telephones, paper, and pencil. In 1974, the center had started utilizing Clearinghouse, a computerized system running on a single, DEC System-20 computer housed at the nearby firm of Bolt, Beranek, and Newman.

All living groups were required to call in periodically to the center to report freshman activity, including which freshmen were currently located at the house, and where those that had just left were headed. R/O switchboard operators took down the data, which was subsequently entered into the Clearinghouse system.

---

12 Id.

•

MIT fraternities averaged around forty people. And each year, they were looking to replace the one-quarter of their members who graduated or left for other reasons. So, on average, each frat was looking for around ten to twelve freshmen.

This meant that the typical fraternity had around thirty brothers who could share in the work for recruiting their ten to twelve prospective pledges. And these thirty were all upperclassmen who had experience in at least one prior rush. Plus, they often had plenty of local alumni who stepped in to lend a hand.

At our new chapter, we were hoping for a pledge class of ten to twelve, at the upper end of the fraternity range. But to recruit these new pledges, we had only ten upperclassmen. And none of us had any rush experience.

We did have R/O Chairman Al Mink in our ranks. This was not necessarily all to our benefit. The IFC council had stringent rules in place to prevent "unfair" rush practices. We really couldn't count on having any special privileges from his position. And his position required him to dedicate a substantial amount of time to that job during the week, leaving us, at times, often with a rush workforce of only nine.

•

The administration, together with the IFC's blessing, did manage to throw at least one bone. And it wasn't sharks with frickin' laser beams.

The two new facilities, ADP and WILG, along with the PKT fraternity, which was reorganizing, were allowed to open booths in the Student Center on Thursday evening, one day before rush officially began for all other fraternities, and to have students visit the house a day earlier than other frats. This early rush helped establish our name in the minds of many freshmen.

From our point of view, rush wasn't just about talking to prospects. We had to plan and staff our logistics. One person was required to staff the phone at all times to field R/O center calls. Someone had to both procure and prepare food to feed both brothers and prospective pledges. And we were never sure just how many we'd have to feed, especially with some of our special events.

Someone had to be available to provide transportation to freshmen that might want to visit. And we had to supply overnight lodging for up to 12 freshmen.

Special destination events, such as picnics, boat rides, and others, enabled fraternities to have exclusive access to a group of potential pledges for the duration of the event, which was always desirable.

But for us, planning and staffing an outing, with only nine or ten people, stretched our resources to their limits. We couldn't dedicate more than half our brothers to any given trip, since a few people would have to stay back at the frat to entertain those who wanted to come by and visit. And we always had to have someone, man our rush desk.

Although our R/O week rush began on Thursday evening, preparation had begun weeks before.

Planning for New Digs

How do you turn a seventy-year-old apartment building into a modern fraternity house?

In the first year, at least, you don't.

We'd hung a sign out in front and did the best with what we had. Our 1977 MIT yearbook page summarized our strategy:

Lambda Phi Chapter of Alpha Delta Phi

"Located Right on Mass Ave"

It appears we knew where our strength lay.

Location, location, location.

But MIT had floated us a promise—by the following year— if we played our cards right—we'd have a brand-new renovated building—one with room to house over fifty brothers, making it potentially one of the largest fraternities on campus.

But how to get there?

MIT hired an architectural firm to plan the renovation—or maybe they got a special deal from Course 4 professors. And they offered us the chance to participate—at least to a limited extent—in the design.

We will be happy to listen to and then ignore your suggestions.

Besides rooms to sleep and study in, what did our fraternity really need?

- A dining room with enough space to feed our eventual fifty-plus brothers each night
- A real kitchen that would allow us to store and prepare food in huge quantities every day. And one that allowed rapid clean-up after meals.
- A living room—a space in which we could hold our chapter meetings, parties, or just hang out. It had to be large enough to hold our entire frat.
- Some sort of outdoor space in which to hold cookouts, and serve as a venue for parties and other events.

According to Corky, planning for the renovation, at least with the City of Cambridge, had begun as early as 1975. Our involvement in the planning started over the summer of 1976 before we had even moved in.

Al, Jon, Bob Wolf, myself, and representatives from WILG, joined MIT housing officials and architects in a series of planning meetings.

Bob didn't like the idea of MIT, or their architects, designing the house, but he did appreciate that they at least made an effort to listen to our inputs.

Most big decisions had already been made. We were to have the largest part of the building some fifty-five percent, with the entrance at 351 Mass Ave.

The women's group would have a smaller section and entered through at the 355 entrance. There were to be no physical connections between the two groups.

At least, not through the building.

•

The building as it existed at that time, was divided into three sections, with a building "peninsula" protruding from the rear of each section. The decision had been made to demolish the upper four floors of the center peninsula.

Bob Wolf recalls that the purpose of the demolition was to open up the rear area of the building and bring additional light into the remaining sections. As it currently stood, many of the rear rooms looked out into the darkness, with of view only of adjacent building walls only a few feet away.

No such demolition could have been accomplished today due to the building's designation in the National Register of Historic Places. However, those were different times.

The center section's demolition created a large outdoor patio area, which fulfilled one of our design goals. The diagram below shows the building's second-floor layout, with the shared patio's entrance door from our soon-to-be living room. [13]

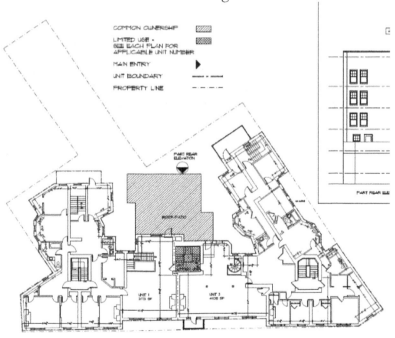

I was supremely interested in the kitchen design, for obvious reasons. Key features included deep sinks for washing huge pots,

_____

[13] A complete set of blueprints for the building can be found at https://lambdaphi.org/wiki.php?page=708

large banks of refrigerators and freezers, a pantry of all dry goods, commercial gas stoves, a large grill, a deep fryer, a meat slicer, and a wonderful commercial dishwasher[*] that could clean, sanitize, and dry an entire rack of dishes seemingly instantaneously.

But the architect saved the best for last.

"The kitchen floor," he informed us, almost breathlessly, "will be a mud job."

For a moment, each of us silently pondered the meaning of such a wondrous thing.

"The mud job," he went on, "will be a seamless epoxy floor, continuing up each wall for several inches, with a drain in the center."

Cleaning up such a floor, we were told, would only require a quick mop, having no seams to catch the dirt. That all sounded wonderful, but not quite as captivating as what we'd been imagining.

•

Jon recalls that WILG had one prospective member who required wheelchair access. The planned ramp, mandated by the City of Cambridge, fit her needs perfectly.

Although WILG's prospective member eventually decided not to join, the ramp proved invaluable for the delivery of food and other items[*] to the building's rear entrance. The first-floor layout section below shows the layout of the two kitchens, patio area, and long "S" ramp.

---

[*] Later, apparently known as the "de-smegmatizer."
[*] Kegs.

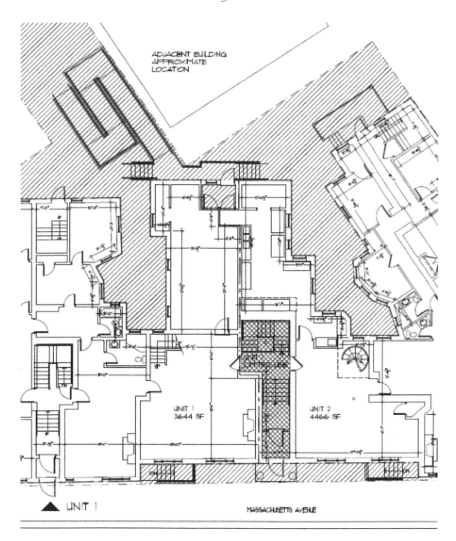

ADJACENT BUILDING
APPROXIMATE
LOCATION

UNIT
LIMITED USE

UNIT 1
3644 SF

UNIT 2
4466 SF

▲ UNIT 1

MASSACHUSETTS AVENUE

At least two other design items were discussed in detail with the architects.

Bob Wolf had seen the Deke house's spiral staircase during his time there and suggested we add one to connect the dining and living rooms. All of us who would be living in the house liked this idea. As I recall, the architects did not. They strongly tried to talk us out of it.

As there doesn't appear to be enough room for the top of a right-angle stairway in our living room, as WILG has on their side, the alternative was no stairway at all, requiring a walk to and from the main stairwell to change floors.

The spiral staircase seemed to go strongly against the architects' design aesthetic. I seem to recall that we went "around and around" with them on this issue, but eventually, they relented.

At least on the stairway issue, we came out on top.

Our spiral staircase ended up being much smaller than the Deke's, and Bob recalls that our tallest members, such as Matt Alves, had to shoehorn themselves into the stairway to head downstairs.

The last major issue was related to windows. We were told that replacing all the old windows would essentially double the cost of the renovations. That wasn't in the MIT budget, which would, in time, become our budget, so we kept the old windows.

This decision would cause us years of window "pains."

Overcrowding Rollercoaster

On Thursday, Sep 9, The Tech newspaper reported that the 1980 class size, instead of 1100, had "only" 1050. The MIT News Office offered up the reasons:

> "MIT had decided last year to set the class size at 1100, but a combination of low "yield" (the fraction of admitted students who accept admission). and a high "melt" (the number of freshmen who accept admission but change their minds during the summer), resulted in the 50 student decline." [14]

In charge of undergraduate housing, Dean Browning was most likely one of the very few in the MIT administration who were pleased over the new numbers. Based on these new class size figures, and the new housing groups, he now estimated dorm overcrowding would be less severe than anticipated.

---

[14] The Tech, Sep 9, 1976, v96-28.

"The reduction in crowding from the projected level was due to a class 50 persons smaller than planned, and to the formation of a new fraternity (ADP) and an Independent Women's Living Group." [15]

In that issue of The Tech, the fraternity rush was being described as "slow, but smooth." Based on the new numbers, earlier estimates of dorm overcrowding were being revised. Burton estimated the number of overcrowded doubles was reduced from 35 down to 20.

An East Campus spokesman estimated only 20 overcrowded freshmen instead of 40, which he described as "normal overcrowding," as opposed to the "abnormal overcrowding" which had been predicted.

And plans to house some freshmen in MacGregor "suite lounges" were canceled.

All-in-all, on September 9, from an MIT housing viewpoint, things were looking up.

•

Five days later, the new headline in The Tech said it all.

"Slow frat rush severely crowds dorms" [16]

The final figures had trickled in. The fraternity rush was not only slow—it was the slowest in ten years. Only 338 freshmen had pledged, as compared to 386 the year before. There were now 108 more students than dormitory "space."

Part of the slow rush was attributed to the fact that dormitories, for the first time, had been allowed to hand out promotional materials during the Freshman Picnic, which was against the current IFC rules for frats.

This early emphasis on dormitories, not apparent in previous years because of the old one-day procedure, will cause a slow rush for some fraternities later in the week.

The IFC was considering changes in the rules for the next year as a counter-measure. But for this year, it would be too late.

---

[15] Ken Browning in The Tech, Sep 9, 1976, v96-28.
[16] The Tech, Sep 14, 1976, v96-29.

Burton re-revised its estimates for the number of triples up to 27. MacGregor now expected anywhere from four to six "suite lounge" doubles. And East Campus presumably entered into "abnormal overcrowding."

And at our chapter, the final rush results were in.

Our First Rush

Having worked like mad to get the house fit for occupants, we now had only a few days to find occupants fit for the house.

A good "fit" works both ways. Our house, and the rooms, were acceptable, but decidedly sub-par when compared to most other frats, or even dorm rooms. Our army surplus desks and chairs wouldn't win any awards for aesthetics, and our previously-owned furniture didn't give anyone a warm and cozy feeling.

Our pledges would need to be aware of this. We had prepared two or three "model" rooms to show to our rush week visitors. Many of the rest of the rooms still needed some major "sprucing up." Those weren't on the official tour.

According to The Tech, the average MIT freshman in 1976, visited 3.7 fraternities, a total of 9.19 times. Why someone felt it was necessary to include three significant digits for that last total will probably be forever unknown.

But the figures themselves *were* significant. Out of the 31 fraternities seeking new members, each freshman (or transfer) realistically only had time to visit a select few.

Over 700 freshmen had arrived Thursday to take advantage

of the new early registration period. For these early arrivals, ADP was afforded a distinct advantage, as summarized in *The Tech*.

> "Groups of freshmen crowd the ADP (AΔΦ), ESG, and Women's Independent Living Group (WILG) booths, keeping open living group options and finding someone to talk to.
>
> In the evening, the early arrivals discover that the fraternities, with the exception of new ADP and WILG, and reorganized PKT (ΦKΘ), are closed, and parties on campus are few and far between." [17]

We had a full day's rush lead over all the established frats. And we'd need it. Every established frat seemed to have some sort of gimmick designed to entice the newcomers:

> There are live bands, a casino. a one-man synthesizer orchestra. film shorts, wine and cheese, pub, lounge, dance, pancake, steak fry, ice cream. cookout, fondue, punch, and shish-kebab parties. [18]

The average frat spent around $2500 ($11,000 in 2021 dollars) to rush the class of 1980, almost exactly $1,000 per head in today's dollars. We had nowhere near that amount. Plus, we had already racked up a lot of bills to get the house, complete with furnishings, ready for occupation. We would be lucky if we were able to spend $500 total on our rush effort, one-fifth of the average of other frats.

So, we limited ourselves to four "major" activities, in addition to the normal breakfasts, lunches, and dinners that freshmen could partake of.

- A beer-tasting party.
- A make-your-own ice cream party.
- A picnic at the Hopkinton State Park.
- A New England seafood dinner.

Jon Cohen recalls heading up the ice cream effort, headlined

[17] The Tech, Sep 9, 1976, v96-28.
[18] Id.

by his famous "apple-cider" ice cream. Ice cream rarely fails to draw a crown, and the effort proved to be a big hit.

Louis Cohen spearheaded the seafood dinner, and came up with our slogan, which we advertised heavily:

Get scrod at ADP!

This was our take on the slogan of a small (at the time) Inman Square seafood market and restaurant, often seen emblazoned on t-shirts around Cambridge at the time:

I got scrod at Legal Seafoods.

Plus, getting "screwed" by the Institute was a popular meme at the time, so our slogan worked in two ways.

Seafood is tough to prepare for large crowds. We procured our fresh "Georges' Bank" scrod wholesale down on Boston's fish pier.

I imagine my conversation with Louis at the time went something like this:

"Why would a bank sell seafood?"

"Seems pretty fishy to me."

"And who's George?"

Each batch of broiled scrod (baby fish, usually cod) and steamed clams had to be prepared fresh, and Louis adeptly handled the task. The chowder, fortunately, could be kept warm in the pot for quite a while.

Getting "scrod" at ADP, it turned out, would prove to be quite popular.

•

Our picnic outing was planned by Bob Anderson. It required the rental of a large 12-14 passenger van to shuttle our crew of freshmen, in addition to the brothers and helpers who facilitated the event.

We also had to prepare food for the picnic—most probably cold cuts, but possibly, hamburgers and hot dogs for the grill.

We did enlist girlfriends to help with this trip, as we needed all hands on deck. We not only had to staff this day trip with enough people to handle all the logistics, but we needed to be able to talk to the prospects as well—otherwise, what's the point?

Even though it was only a relatively small outing, it consumed a large fraction of our small group's manpower.

Well, nobody said this rush was going to be a picnic.

I drove the passenger van, filled with freshmen, to and from the park. The back end of the van weaved unsteadily with our full load. The rearmost passengers were complaining about getting carsick.

We stopped at a gas station, with the intent of adding pressure to the rear tires. I located the tire pump, pulled forward, and shifted into reverse to back the rear of the van closer to the air pump. At that instant, a Masshole driver zipped in between the van and the pump, beating me to the air hose.

What the fuck?

He ignored my protestations, and being under severe time pressure (as well as tire pressure), we had to take off, unfulfilled. I drove very carefully, taking all corners slow and easy. I was carrying precious cargo.

Everyone's future.

Day trips were important tools for during a rush. They kept our prime prospects away from other fraternities for a good chunk of the day. To prevent abuse, there were rules in place on how long outings could be, but we took full advantage to make sure we had the best chance to keep our top choices.

Decisions Made in a Rush

On Thursday, Friday, and Saturday evenings of rush week, the ten of us met in our dining/meeting room to review the candidates of the day.

Closed-door sessions only.

Upstairs, our allotted contingent of freshmen and transfers lay in our open rooms, presumably sleeping.

We had relied on the much-maligned "Hello, my name is _____" stickers to associate names with faces, and most importantly, to associate them to the personal impressions we had of each candidate. We wore the stickers, too, so the candidates would know who they were talking to. We like to joke about the stickers, but they worked.

At one point, I had to venture out to a store in Harvard Square to purchase some desperately-needed rush item. As I stepped up to the counter, the young female clerk looked me in the eye.

"Hi, Tony."

A baffled expression came over my face.

Did I know this person? Had I met her sometime last year?

For the life of me, I couldn't place her.

Her quick downward glance caused me to follow her gaze. I grimaced. I was still sporting my sticker.

She smirked.

It was a very loud smirk.

Hello, my name is Tony. And I'm a dork.

●

It's hard to recall how we kept track of our potential bids. One thing is clear, it wasn't on a computer. Trying to recall who-was-who, after seeing fifty or more freshman, in addition to working all day, was no mean feat. Taking a Polaroid picture of each person, and then writing their name on it would have been a splendid idea and one that we seemed to have missed.

Sunday was a day of bad weather, canceling many frats' outdoor day trips, in addition to keeping many freshmen from venturing far from the dorms. This was thought to be another reason for the overall slow fraternity rush.

Fortunately, our trip had been on Saturday, and the weather had been fine.

●

Jon Cohen recalls a memory from one rush, most likely the following year's, but still relevant to any rush. One prospect he encountered was smoking a cigarette. Jon informed him that there was no smoking at that location. The response—blowing smoke in Jon's face—instantly put him on Jon's shit list.

At the night's meeting, everybody seemed to like this guy. Jon was astonished.

"Wait a minute," he asked. "Who's actually met this guy?"

Only one person raised their hand. Everyone else was passing on secondhand or thirdhand opinions—the rush week equivalent of the game of "telephone."

After Jon's tale was recounted, the guy was not extended an offer. The lesson was clear—only make a recommendation if you've met the person first-hand.

●

Adrian recalls that our rush discussions often went like this:
"What do you think of this guy?"
"He's nice"
"What about this guy?"
"He's nice"
After two or three more "nice" evaluations, that word was banned from the rush meeting.

All I want to know is 'in, or out.' No more mister nice guys!

•

We had had a lot of visitors during the first three days of rush week. We asked each candidate how serious they were about our house. But that question comes with a caveat, as the savviest freshmen are going to tell you what you want to hear, maximizing their chance of getting bids from several houses.

As a consequence, we tried to be upfront with our top prospects and essentially asked them not to jerk us around if they weren't serious, as it was our first year and we didn't have a lot of room for error.

After all, this *was* our first rodeo.

After three nights of deliberation, we decided to extend bids to a total of twelve freshmen and transfers.

Ten pledges would put us at a house size of twenty, more or less ideal for our current accommodations. We could squeeze in up to two more by combining one of our larger singles into a double and by utilizing one "iffy" pass-through room that was less than ideal.

•

Rush bids couldn't go out until 8 am on Sunday. At that instant, every frat would start issuing bids to the top prospects that were staying at their houses, and would also begin calling the R/O center to contact prospects who were staying in the dorm or other frats.

We felt it was important to be the first frat to extend a bid, if at all possible.

We knew time was of the essence. We woke up all of our candidates at 8 am sharp and extended offers to the sometimes groggy students. We called up the remainder of the twelve on the phone and extended bids and attempted to get them back to the frat for another visit and schmooze session.

And then we waited. And waited.

No offers could be accepted before Monday morning.

We had a good idea about some of our choices, but, more than likely, these candidates were going to be in demand from other frats, also. We were going to have to wait twenty-four hours, at least, to gauge the success of our first effort.

One by one, we heard back from those we had bid. By Monday evening, the complete results were in.

By the end of the day, every one of the twelve offers had been accepted. We'd hit our target on the first try.

Jon recalls that we were one of the first houses to close rush. As mentioned, many other houses experienced a slower-than-normal rush. Our summer mailings, along with the Thursday early exposure had given us a big boost.

Plus, we did it all on a shoestring budget.

•

My suggestion for the pledge class name—"Cheaper by the Dozen," to commemorate our bargain-basement rush budget, was not met with uniform acclaim by the members of said class.

They went with "Dirty Dozen," instead.

Heathens!

Our twelve pledges, plus the original ten, pushed our house capacity to the limit. One pledge, Loren Kohnfelder, had to make do with a "walk-through" room. Decidedly sub-optimal.

Perhaps the number of people tramping through his room spurred on Loren's efforts to develop a practical means to secure his information. [19]

Our new pledges significantly extended our geographic diversity. In addition to two international students, three were from the Western States and one additional Midwesterner. Two upperclassmen were part of the pledge class.

And lastly, our new group contained one "animal."

---

[19] https://dspace.mit.edu/handle/1721.1/15993

Rush – Views From the Other Side

Tom Burgmann answered the phone in the dorm room where he was housed during rush week.

The voice on the other side asked if another student was around.

"Nope, not here," Tom replied.

After a brief pause, Al Mink switched gears.

"Well, how about you? Would you like to come to the Alpha Delta Phi seafood dinner tonight?"

As an upperclassman transfer, Tom was aware that it was extremely unlikely that he'd get accepted into the already overcrowded dormitory system, but he was allowed to participate in the fraternity rush.

When he'd checked into the student activities center, Fern Crandall, the helpful APO assistant, had suggested looking into fraternities for housing.

Tom scoffed. He was familiar with frats at the University of Toronto, where he was transferring from.

"What, do I look like some sort of beer-guzzling jock?" he thought to himself, almost loud enough for Fern to hear.

She could see Tom had a bit of an attitude. But then, she kind of liked men with attitudes.

"Fraternities here are different from other colleges," she added, "They're all filled with smart people, and they're a big part of the housing solution. It might be a good alternative for you."

Never one to not listen and learn, Tom checked out some frats. He'd already been courted by another Back Bay fraternity, but he'd seen their communal sleeping arrangements and wasn't entirely thrilled.

At this point, he was seriously considering signing on to share an apartment in Somerville.

"Sure," he replied to Al. "Seafood sounds great."

•

Tom was immediately impressed. Not so much by the physical building, which was sub-par, or the people, who were decidedly *not* sub-par, but by the potential.

"You're going to be a part of building this thing. Not a new building, but a brand-new chapter."

Being a part of a team that was creating new traditions and shaping the culture of the fraternity appealed to him in a big way. There was never any doubt that ADP was his first choice.

Rob Mandel even loaned him a copy of a book to read during rush— "Marathon Man." After that, Tom had only one further question.

Is it safe?

•

Todd Hubing recalls that, during rush week, our chapter had a lot of women around. Whether these were girlfriends of the first ten members or members and candidates of WILG is not clear, but the presence of women was a definite plus.

He also noted the relaxed atmosphere at our house, which, given the amount of activity that had gone on immediately prior to the rush, was probably the result of everyone being totally worn out.

Todd had a bid from another frat but decided that our chapter suited his needs the best.

We agreed.

•

Matt Alves indicated that other frats he'd visited were looking for specific types of personalities, in contrast to our chapter where we were not focused on any particular "type" of pledge. We didn't have a fraternity "label," and we weren't looking for one, other than being a nice place to live.

He recalls that we were a bunch of regular people.

Well, as regular as you get for MIT students.

•

Andy Bronstein liked the "startup" atmosphere of our chapter. He must have because our facilities definitely weren't the best at the time. He and Matt ended up being sandwiched into the only 'single-room' double in the house.

Andy recalls that we were just a nice group of people.

Andy has always been extremely perceptive.

Our location was another plus. Near restaurants, pubs, Central Square shops, and the "T" station, we were unique among all MIT fraternities.

He may have noticed the "Campus House of Pizza" just a block or two away from the frat, on the way to the campus, which he later recalled as having the best pizza in the city, even though its Greek owners appeared to be bickering any time anyone entered.

•

Bob Glatz was housed in the East Campus dorm during R/O week and quickly determined that that was not the kind of residential situation in which he wished to find himself for any length of time.

After visiting a few frats, he felt like our chapter seemed like a good fit, both ways, and he liked the people that he had gotten to talk to.

It didn't hurt that ADP seemed like a phenomenal bargain compared to the other housing choices he'd seen. While he could see that facilities weren't the best—at least for the present—Bob appreciated that living in the house would make MIT's high financial costs a little easier to tolerate.

•

"You're not supposed to be here."

These were the first words Jeff Thiemann heard from the MIT admissions office after his arrival into this country.

The son of Lutheran missionaries, Jeff graduated from high school in Ethiopia, and applied to MIT and Columbia, in addition to a Lutheran college in Iowa.

He thought about applying to Harvard, but once he received early acceptance to MIT, all thoughts of other institutions were summarily dismissed.

Communications between Jeff and MIT had taken place primarily by way of telegram, and there were quite a few challenges along the way, including a requirement to take the "English as a Second Language" test, which was eventually waived for this Houston-born, native English speaker.

But MIT still apparently wanted Jeff to come two days early for the foreign students' orientation, so Jeff flew from Addis-Ababa to Boston, arriving on the prescribed date.

MIT quickly realized that Jeff wasn't a foreign student in need of any special orientation.

"You need to find a place to stay until R/O week starts two days from now."

Having no money for a hotel, Jeff finally convinced them to let him stay in a dorm.

That was awfully nice of them.

With two days to kill, Jeff embarked on a walking tour of Cambridge, and eventually happened upon our chapter house.

Al Mink was outside, doing some work-week painting.

Jeff struck up a conversation, and before long, Al invited him in for lunch, which at the time, consisted of a bologna sandwich.[*]

Never one to pass up free food, Jeff accepted Al's offer. Inside he met Adrian and Rob Mandel and had a chance to get to know some of our members in a relaxed setting.

---

[*] Clearly, the author didn't plan that lunch menu.

Al, never one to let an opportunity pass by, recruited Jeff to help in the painting effort.

From his very first encounter, Jeff left his mark on our chapter.

Given that he'd already participated in our work week, it was not surprising that Jeff came by our fraternity two days later.

He was impressed with what seemed to be a serious, but fun group, who stressed the importance of being well-rounded.

The chance to begin on the ground floor was one of the biggest plusses. Little did he know how true this would be, as his first-year accommodations were in a front, ground-floor double, where he was treated to the sounds of semi-trucks backing up to the nearby Junior Mint factory at 4:30 every morning.

Once again—be careful what you wish for.

To Jeff, the young startup chapter helped inspire him to envision "dreams of what we could become." His dreams were realized just a few years later when Jeff moved from the office of house president to the real seat of power—food steward in charge of menu planning.

Meeting Everyone

"The meeting shall come to order"

Our first house meeting was underway, the eminent Adrian Zuckerman, presiding.

Twenty-two pledges, from both pledge classes, filled the small dining room.

Steve Ofsthun held a fresh new copy of "Roberts Rules of Order," obtained at the MIT Coop, just for this very purpose.

Although, with four "Roberts" between the two pledge classes, it wasn't clear why we even needed the book.

Dinner was simmering in the kitchen upstairs.

Chile con carne, in a huge pot.

For some reason, we'd decided to hold our first chapter meeting immediately before our first full house dinner. Although a good idea on paper, this neglected one particularly important aspect—someone had to cook.

And at this moment, that job fell upon me.

I didn't want to miss our very first house meeting, so I had attempted to keep things "simmering" in the kitchen until the meeting was over.

For the freshman pledges, this was a time for them to begin settling in. They'd chosen, or been assigned to, their rooms. As far as I recall, no one had serious issues, although Andy and Matt had been crammed into what was really a single room, and Loren's room was decidedly sub-optimal.

We were at the upper limits of our capacity. But no one seemed to be complaining.

•

Our first meeting was also a chance for everyone to get to know everyone else, and just to take a breath.

Rush statistics were reviewed. We patted ourselves on the back for a superb first rush.

Adrian gushed over the new pledges.

"This is by far the best new pledge class I've ever seen," he beamed.

Of course, it was the *only* new pledge class he'd ever seen.

But that didn't stop the new members, and everyone else, from feeling pretty good about our overall efforts at the time.

And it *was* a good group.

The ten of us had learned from our alumni organizers to snap fingers in place of applause. Snapping soon became an ingrained habit, but at first, it always elicited a grin from the new pledges, and any guests attending our dinners for the first time.

•

Most officers had little to report, other than announcing that they would be working on plans shortly to present at the next meeting.

One of the biggest decisions was how to approach food preparation. It was agreed to assign teams of three people to cook dinner six nights a week. Each team would cook, serve, and clean. I was tasked with coming up with the schedule.

Saturday, everyone would fend for themselves. Brothers would be free to cook for themselves or heat any leftovers, if available. Breakfast and lunch were 'make-your-own.' We provided ample food for both.

We also had to determine what we'd charge for dues. This was a difficult job at first, with no history, and no established budgets to work from. More than likely, we made a rough estimate, with a caveat that we might have to make some revisions down the road.

Russ went over the complicated process to be utilized if anyone had problems with their rooms or furniture.

"Let me know."

Bob Wolf noted that he was starting to gather pledge materials. The first pledge class would have to train itself.

Who trains the trainer?

About that time, someone noticed something a little out of the ordinary.

"What's that smell?"

"It's smoke!"

I dashed upstairs, following the hazy trail into the kitchen. It was the chili. Great puffs of gray smoke belched from the pot at regular intervals.

So much for simmering.

The chili was salvageable—for the most part. That is if you like a strong, smoky, ashtray flavor. Someone commented that it should have been called "chile con char-ne."

For once, I was not amused by clever wordplay.

The carbonized residue on the bottom of our new pot took quite a bit of soaking, scraping, and elbow grease, to remove.

From that time on, there was just one rule that I insisted on.

No house meetings before dinner.

•

Left-to-right – Loren Kohnfelder, Tony Pelham, Russ Kalis, Bob Wolf, Cliff Kelly, Jon Cohen, Pete Arndt, Matt Alves, Chris King, Tom Burgmann, Andy Bronstein, Carl Heinzl (front), Louis Cohen, Adrian Zuckerman, Steve Ofsthun Jeff Thiemann, Rob Mandel, Bob Glatz, Al Mink, Todd Hubing, Bob Anderson, Bret Hartman.

Food for Thought

There's an old expression regarding the military:

An army travels on its stomach.

Our chapter was not much different. Meals are a vital part of fraternity life, and not just for the food alone. The daily evening meals are the one time each day when the brothers assemble, so they become an important part of the social life of a chapter.

Many fraternities hire a full-time chef to prepare lunches and dinners. Fraternity chefs plan and coordinate menus, compile lists of foods for purchase, and, of course, cook the food.

All this comes, not surprisingly, at a cost. A full-time chef is expensive. The salary and benefits for the chef are passed on directly to each brother, in terms of higher dues. For a small chapter, such as ours in its first year, the cost of a full-time chef was prohibitive. A decade or more down the road, when the chapter house had over fifty brothers, the house did decide to do just that.

Another possibility would be to pay house members to cook. This is what our chapter did, starting in our second year.

The cost of hiring house members to cook would be much less than a full-time chef would require, and the impact on annual dues was correspondingly less.

•

However, there was one more option. It was by far the least costly, at least in terms of dollars spent. But it had some other costs, which, as we discovered, were not at all trivial.

In the first year of the chapter, we decided to split cooking duties among all brothers. With twenty-two brothers, we had enough people for six teams of three brothers each. Each team was on duty one night each week, to prepare, serve, and clean up afterward.

As the food steward, I was exempt from the regular cooking schedule, given the fact that I needed to perform all the "behind-the-scenes" work associated with making sure at least some food managed to make it into each brother's stomach, every single day.

Most of the teams had little-to-no cooking experience whatsoever, and none had experience cooking for such a large group.

Rather than being thrown from the proverbial frying pan into the fire, our initial group was being "thrown" from the classroom into the frying pan.

There was a significant learning curve, one in which food quality suffered. And not everyone had the aptitude, or the desire to cook. For some groups, the meals never seemed to get much better.

•

The food steward's work, as I found out, was never-ending. In the first semester, my duties included:
- Planning the menus two weeks in advance.
- Compiling a list of food ingredients necessary for the planned meals, a week or so in advance.
- Inventorying the current stock of food/kitchen items.
- Calling each vendor each week (or as needed) and making the order. We had separate IFC-approved

vendors that we used for:
- groceries
- meats
- dairy/eggs
- seafood
- produce
- bakery

- Receiving the orders when delivered, and verifying that all the order was filled (some of the drivers liked to try to "short" us).
- Stocking the delivered goods in the pantry or refrigerators.
- Rotating the stock and disposing of old or expired food.
- Supervising each of the cooking groups on how to cook the recipe for the night's meal.
- Make sure the stock of kitchen/dining room equipment, dishes, glasses, silverware was adequate.
- Making sure we were within allowed budgets.

That much responsibility, as I later came to find out, was almost a guaranteed 'recipe' for burnout.

The Finances

At the time of this writing (2021), one 1976 dollar had the equivalent purchasing power of somewhere around $4.70 in 2021 dollars.

For purposes of clarity, I'll include the 2021 dollar equivalents in parentheses for all figures throughout this book. If you're reading this book in 2050, you'll have to do your own, updated, calculations—but you'll also probably have a brain implant that will handle this for you without any effort.

Brother Jon Cohen, a Course 15-3 Management Science major, was the treasurer for our entire first year, and also, somewhat surprisingly, for the second year.

Surprisingly, because the job of treasurer, especially in the days before computers, was one of the most time-intensive of all jobs at the frat. Receipts had to be accounted for, bills had to be paid, checks had to be written and mailed, budgets had to be reconciled, accounts had to be set up at various vendors such as hardware stores, food suppliers, furniture outlets, the phone company and more, and the financial books had to be kept.

Jon had some guidance – he met regularly with Alpha Delt

alumnus Bob McKelvey, who showed him how to set up the financial books for the ADP board meetings, including how to prepare an income statement and balance sheet, and how to keep a financial journal.

•

Our best recollections are that first-year dues were around $1,600 ($7,500) for the academic year, Exact figures are hard to come by for this era of pen and paper.

Our rent to MIT likely occupied a much higher percentage of our budget than in later years. This was partially compensated by having no expenditures for deferred maintenance, which was not necessary for our first year, as the building was being renovated, and in the several years that followed, due to the newness of the renovated building.*

As a basis of comparison, representative dormitory costs at the time ranged from $1,000 to $1,200 ($4,600 to $5,600) per year. Dormitory meal plan cost varied according to the number of meals provided. The full-blown plan, including 19 meals a week, ran $1,130 ($5,300) for two terms. So, room and board at a dorm could easily run over $2,600 ($10,000) for the school year.

Other frats offered a variety of food plans. At PIKA, where house members were paid to cook seven nights a week, and an open, stocked kitchen was available at all hours, the food plan costs $530 ($2,500) for the academic year, about half the cost of the full-blown dorm plan.

At $1,600 total for room and board, our dues were substantially less than a dorm plan. Of course, we didn't pay anyone to do the cooking, but we did always have an open stocked kitchen.

•

We needed at least one house phone. At the time, a business line was considerably more expensive than a personal line. Jon ended up getting the phone in his own name to save money.*

---

* Brother Steve Bergstein correctly notes that a properly run organization needs a plan for deferred maintenance.

* Eventually, the phone came to be in the name of Alferd D. Peters.

AT&T balked at having multiple lines in one person's name, so we initially ended up with only a single line for the entire frat.

Local calls were free, long-distance calls were extra. We had a signup sheet by the phone to record long-distance calls, as the calls could easily cost over a dollar per minute at today's prices, and needed to be reimbursed, adding to the treasurer's monthly chores.

At least one brother racked up hundreds of dollars of long-distance phone charges each month during our first year.

AT&T loved long-distance relationships.

As mentioned earlier, the average MIT fraternity in 1977 spent around $2,500 ($12,000) for their rush, which yielded 11 pledges, on average, so the going rate for a single pledge averaged around $230 ($1070).[20] We had spent nowhere near this amount on our first rush.

It was clear that our pledges had provided a much better-than-average return on investment.

The treasurer's job was time-consuming, often thankless, never-ending, and at one point in Jon's second year, overwhelming. It was also a vitally important component of the ongoing viability of the fraternity.

Establishing the initial financial structure and the precedents for the house finances was an order-of-magnitude more difficult task than simply taking over the position when such procedures and systems were already in place.

Some of the earliest sacrifices toward getting the fraternity on a sound footing were performed by our first treasurer.

---

[20] The Tech, Sep 2, 1977, v97-29

Living with WILG

The general plan was that we would occupy one-third of the building during the first year, specifically the third of the building at 351 Mass Ave. Our fraternity would occupy the lower two-and-a-half floors, and the yet-unnamed women's group would occupy the upper two-and-a-half floors.

The women's groups' decision to take the upper floors was, in part, a security consideration. We provided a buffer through which any possible interlopers would have to pass, giving WILG members one extra margin of safety.

We were more than happy to serve as protectors of the women's group, as the floor assignments seemed to be advantageous to us in several ways.

First, we didn't have to trek up three or four flights of stairs to reach our rooms, and second, it allowed us to claim the basement for use as common areas.

Annexing the basement seemed like the logical thing to do. It was the natural order of things—our manifest destiny.

Fraternities need Lebensraum, too.

The most important basement common room was the area that we transformed into our first-year dining/meeting room.

I don't recall any discussions regarding which group would "own" the basement common areas, or what the women would do for their dining needs, but, sad to say, those thoughts never crossed our minds.

Perhaps, as a concession, we did allow them to use our washers and dryers in the basement.

As long as they had exact change.

•

At some point, we came up with a new name with which to refer to WILG residents— "The Wiggles." I recall that this scrambled acronym was my idea. I am not proud of this fact. I am also reasonably sure that everyone else in the house believes that they were the ones who originally coined this term.

Even at the time, we knew the name was condescending and somewhat misogynistic. But over time, it just became the name we used, with no ill-meaning intended. However, we were generally careful not to use the term around the WILG members.

For some reason, they didn't seem to care for it.

•

Not only were the women independent, but some of the WILG members were fiercely so. They tolerated our presence, but it was clear from the start that it was a relationship based on necessity, and one that could end as soon as their half of the building was completed.

Other members, however, seemed to accept, or even appreciate the presence of studly fraternity men *(along with the rest of us)* sharing a portion of the building. At the end of rush, they even hosted a joint "Get to know your neighbor party" with the frat.

Mr. Rogers would have approved.

One Steward to Feed Them All

"Makes four to six servings."

The greatest lie of all time was not told by the Devil, but by Irma Rombauer, in her work, "Joy of Cooking."

Each week, I'd pick out six recipes from the renowned cookbook to use in upcoming meals the following week.

The recipes were sized for a "typical" American family of four.

The only problem was, Irma's hypothetical family members didn't seem to eat like normal people, much less like ravenous college students.

Scaling up all ingredient quantities by a factor of twenty-two-fourths was simple enough for our cooks to figure out on their own, at least the ones who hadn't needed to take "Physics for Poets."

It was *not* the correct solution.

Three servings per person, minimum.

I drilled this mantra into every cooking team before every

meal. I made them repeat it back to me.

"How many servings do we make?"

"At least three servings per person. Scale-up all recipes by a factor of sixteen."

"Correct!" I affirm. "Everything gets scaled! One teaspoon of salt becomes sixteen."

I watched as their eyes widened at the absurdity of such a notion.

Sixteen teaspoons of salt!

"However," I'd continue, "always double-check your math! Seasoning errors are usually irreversible. Measure twice— pour once!"

The fact that the cookbooks used English units made scaling even more error-prone.

Where was the metric system when we needed it?

There are 48 teaspoons in a cup, so in our hypothetical example, we'd need one-third cup of salt.

One-third cup of salt!

"And don't dump it in all at once. Add a fraction, then taste. You can always add in more salt, but you can't 'unsalt' the mashed potatoes."

•

Despite my best efforts, we had more than a few misfires over the course of the first year.

I was trying to teach undergrads, many of whom never cooked *at all*, to cook for twenty-two students, using a kitchen that was sized to produce meals for three or four people.

Bob Wolf recalls being overwhelmed by the sheer quantity of ingredients required to feed our small army of twenty-two. He also learned that there was more than one way to cook spaghetti.

The recipe called for onions, which are usually chopped, then sauteed, before adding to the sauce. According to Bob's recollection, Al Mink would just chuck whole onions into the pot of sauce and let them cook.

Well, it did save time.

Hopefully, he peeled them first.

•

Once a week I would create the menus for the next week, then use the menus to compile the lists of ingredients into specific orders from each of the vendors.

The grocery vendor had a huge line-printed listing that comprised their "catalog." Each item had various "qualities" at different price levels. I once ordered the cheapest cans of applesauce. After serving up the green slimy mixture with dinner, I complained to the customer rep over the phone.

"Oh yeah," he remarked, "that kind's only used in Chinese restaurants. You probably shouldn't order that."

Thanks a lot.

Canned goods generally came in huge "number 10" cans, seven-inch diameter behemoths that each held over three quarts. These cans became the staple of our kitchen pantry. We had an "industrial" can opener, with a giant crank, which was bolted to one countertop, which could open one of these babies in just a few seconds.

Sometimes the appropriate quantities to order were hard to judge. I once (and only once) ordered a one-pound box of bay leaves for seasoning. I found out that one pound of bay leaves is quite a lot— it arrived in an enormous box. I think these bay leaves lasted until Decade Three.

Figuring that everyone would like some tea, now and then, I also ordered tea bags. The 1-oz size seemed right for us thirsty college boys. What arrived was a case of gigantic tea bags, each the size of a woman's pocketbook, sized to make five gallons of tea at a time.

Looks like we'll be drinking lots of iced tea this semester.

At one point, I thought people might enjoy black bean soup to heat up for their lunches. So, I ordered a case of Campbell's black bean soup, in normal-sized cans. As it turned out, nobody liked Campbell's black bean soup. Two years later, when I left the fraternity, they gave me a farewell present—the remaining cans of black bean soup.

Could I have some bay leaves with that?

•

The food budget I worked with was by far the largest discretionary budget in the house, so it was important to stay within its constraints. This affected the types of meals we could offer. Hello, spaghetti and meatballs, casseroles, and a perennial favorite, Hungarian goulash.

Expensive meats, like steaks, were only planned infrequently, generally for the special Friday meals when brothers could invite guests.

I recall at one point that our milk consumption was threatening to take us over budget. Milk was served with dinner meals. Since most people just poured one glass for the meal, I hypothesized that consumption could be reduced by ordering smaller-sized glasses (but not too small, which would lead people to refill their glass, increasing consumption).

After plan implementation, milk consumption fell dramatically. The budget was saved!

It was a 'pour' plan, but it worked!

The Lease

One truth is nearly universal—financials are dull. Unless, perhaps, when they pertain to you personally.

The lease of the chapter's building at 351 Mass Ave did pertain to everyone who lived at the frat, since—especially in the earliest years—it constituted a major part of our dues.

MIT purchased the building in 1976 from its Northgate subsidiary. Total cost, including renovations, totaled roughly one million dollars.

Cue Dr. Evil voiceover.

The MIT President's report from 1975/76 was cheerfully optimistic regarding the project's prospects.

> Project cost, including purchase price but not including provisions for parking, is projected at $1 million or $10,000 per bed for 100 beds. The enthusiasm of the groups and the availability of a good facility make success appear likely.

The building was allotted 55/45 to ADP/WILG, and ADP's portion of the building cost was deemed to be $606k ($2.8M in

2021 dollars)

Interest rates in 1976 hovered around eight percent, or even higher. A quick calculation indicates that interest payments alone at an eight percent rate would amount to $48k/year ($225K)!

With 22 brothers in 1976, paying interest-only at the prevailing rates would have cost each brother $10,000 in equivalent 2021 dollars. This would have been a non-starter.

So, how were we—and MIT—able to pull this off?

Government to the rescue!

The answer, in a word, was HUD. MIT was able to purchase the property with a three-percent HUD loan. As the President's 1977-78 report put it:

> However, the Federal government reopened the College Housing Program through HUD with priorities defined in such a way as to make this project appear of high priority. Accordingly, we applied for and received a Federal loan under terms of 3 percent-40 years to provide the required permanent financing.

The wording of this statement is quite remarkable. One wonders how long it took the report writer to come up with the convoluted brilliance of: "with priorities defined in such a way as to make this project appear of high priority."

•

A quick loan amortization calculation on a 40-year loan on $606K at a 3% interest rate yields an annual payment of $26,000.

That's more like it!

But there's more! MIT didn't want to commit to a lease/purchase with ADP or WILG until each organization proved itself to be viable.

The President's 1975/76 annual report continued:

> In late May, the decision was made for M. I. T. to purchase the building, renovate it to meet the needs of those groups while renting them some space in the building, and to sell each group its house when work was complete, *and the groups thoroughly established.*

In other words, to mitigate its risk, MIT decided to charge ADP and WILG rent for the first few years until they were established, at which time a sale/lease would then be enacted.

MIT could easily afford this due to the exceedingly favorable 3% HUD loan terms.

Charging rent equal to interest-only at 3% would have been $18K ($85K) annually, still too high for the first year, with a chapter size of only 22 brothers, but doable when the chapter size hit 45 or more the following years.

Thus, it's highly likely that, at least for the first year, MIT reduced the rental charges to be in line with the fraction of the building that was occupied. It also appears that they subsidized our utility costs during that time, and most likely, property taxes and insurance also.

But it gets even better!

•

By 1983, MIT had finally determined the Lambda Phi chapter of ADP, and WILG, were "thoroughly established." The sale— actually a lease with a one-dollar purchase option after 38 years, was about to be formalized, with a term retroactively starting from 1982.

The years from 1976 through 1982 were the era of hyperinflation in the US. The inflation rate for the period averaged over 8%, hitting a peak of 13% in 1980. Locking in a 3% loan in 1976 dollars meant that by the time the lease was enacted in 1983, the true cost of the loan had already been reduced by some 70% due to the intervening six to seven years of unprecedented inflation.

In 1983, MIT committed to charging ADP an annual lease payment of $26,131 ($68K) for 38 years, a raw total strikingly close to the original HUD loan amortization figure.

The chart below shows the effects of inflation on the lease amount in equivalent 2020 dollars, the year the lease-purchase option was exercised. The chart values, also showing the six years before 1982, show just how much the effects of the high inflation

of that period affected the true dollar cost of the lease.

What's immediately apparent is how much less the chapter had to pay in real dollars in each succeeding year of the house lease.

Yay, inflation!

•

There were a few more costs associated with the lease, however. A charge for furniture and fixtures of $51k ($132K) was to be amortized over a 15-year term at an annual cost of roughly $5k ($13k), adding twenty percent to the annual lease payments.

The furniture and fixtures capital cost seems high, but these likely included the costs of expensive commercial kitchen equipment.

The sprinkler system cost another $18k, amortized over 25 years at an annual cost of $1K ($2.6K).

Also, the lease required we fund a repair and replacement maintenance reserve account of $52K ($135K) at $3.4K/year ($9K) until the reserve account total was reached after 15 years, and then replenished if maintenance expenditures were incurred.

This additional cost pushed the total lease payments to a total of around $35K/year ($91K) for the first 15 years.

•

The lease was signed on December 30, 1983, with a lease term commencing retroactively from May 1, 1982, and expiring on June 30, 2020. It was signed by Friends of Alpha Delta Phi President, Adrian Zuckerman, and Treasurer, Kevin Ossler.

A separate agreement that also included a provision that shared costs with WILG, primarily utilities, had to be suitably worked out between the groups.

Thirty-eight years was so far into the future that most of us could only imagine what the world would be like at such a time the lease term ended.

Like the futuristic Jetson family, some of us thought that by 2020 we'd have flying cars and robotic vacuum cleaners and that we'd work at jobs where we'd simply push buttons all day and come home, exhausted.

Fat chance!

But 2020 eventually surfaced, and not surprisingly, ADP decided to exercise its one-dollar purchase option. In actuality, the purchase wasn't quite so simple, as former Corporation President Steven Bergstein noted:

> There was some real cost involved – [ADP] and WILG had to hire (separate) attorneys to draw up a bunch of documents to create the condo association, create the right deeds and other documents, and then file the right paperwork with the Registry of Deeds.

We also hired an architect to draw up floor plans for the entire building, which she did beautifully.

And for some reason, in the final settlement statement, that "one dollar" never actually showed up.

Social Life

"Toga, Toga, Toga."

Forever memorialized in 1978's Animal House, the fraternity toga party can be traced back at least to the 1950s.

We didn't have any toga parties in our first year, but that didn't mean we didn't have any social life.

Corky Corcoran used our house as his base for several months while he worked with other New York and New England chapters. While he was helping us startup, he was also working on reopening the Columbia chapter in New York City.

According to Corky's recollection, he had one overriding goal for our chapter—to bring us up to the "Big Ten" levels for social interactions that he was used to at the Minnesota chapter.

Although initially skeptical, after a few months of effort, he was quite satisfied with the results. He recalls several "recruiting" trips to Wellesley College to entice women to come over for one of our planned, or perhaps, spur-of-the-moment, events.

•

Bob Anderson, our first social director, preferred to plan

somewhat more sophisticated events that a typical fraternity might host. His favorite was the champagne-tasting event. Bob seemed to have unlimited connections, and he appeared to know women everywhere, but he had several strong connections at Wellesley.

He provided us with an "in" at the women's college—helping incoming students unload their belongings and set up their rooms, where we might just happen to mention: "Oh, by the way, would you like to come to our party this weekend?"

On another occasion, Bob set up some of our members on a group blind date with an equal number of Wellesley women. According to accounts, Rob Mandel drew the worst of the selection. Bob Anderson later apologized for this "moose-take."

Jon Cohen recalls that at one point, Bob rounded up "twenty-two women," and a school bus for an all-fraternity day trip to Cape Cod. It remains unclear how and where Bob managed to find such an abundance of women, but I have yet to note any complaints from anyone in our first two pledge classes.

•

Andy noted that one of the few drawbacks to a brand new fraternity was that there weren't a lot of older brothers with cars and connections.

To compensate, several members of the pledge class became adept at finding ways to get into various parties. On one occasion, Bob drove several pledges out to a party at Wellesley. There was a cover charge to get in.

Not to worry, they went around back and found some of the extra beer kegs reserved for later use. They simply began carrying the kegs into the house, being taken as workers. Once in, they stayed.

Cover charge – bypassed!

•

Cliff Kelly was our social director for the second semester. Cliff was so successful at engaging our fraternity member's social life, that he ended up getting engaged himself.

Cliff married and left the house after only a year.

Thiemann' Up

"If you go off to MIT, you can kiss me goodbye."

Pam Wolf's boyfriend had issued the "ultimate" ultimatum. She went.

Coming from a small town of only 5,000 in upstate New York, Pam was excited, and not a little intimidated, to be going to school in the Boston/Cambridge area. Her ex-boyfriend did not share in her excitement.

During rush, she attended several women's events, including looking at WILG, but eventually settled in the Burton Dormitory.

She had, however, met some friends who'd joined WILG, and at the end of rush week, she was invited, with her new roommate Helen, to come to the ADP/WILG "Get to know your neighbor" party, our chapter's first-ever joint party with WILG, and probably our first party of any type.

The party was held on the fifth floor in one of the women's group's lounges.

•

Jeff Thiemann immediately noticed the cute blonde at the

party, and he walked over and introduced himself. They talked over a big bowl of popcorn, but the loud music from one brother's brand new stereo setup made it difficult for them to hear one another.

Jeff suggested they head out to the fire escape balcony to chat, but Pam declined—she had heard about these "big-city" boys with their clever schemes.

They ended up sitting on one of the stairway landings, where, at least, Pam reasoned, there would be other people around who could be called on to defend her against any of Jeff's advances, if needed.

When it became time for Pam to leave, Jeff declared that he would walk her home to Burton. Pam was wary.

I just met this guy.

She excused herself and found her roommate.

"We've got to go, *now!*" she told Helen. "There's a guy here who wants to walk me home!"

Pam and Helen quickly collected their things and headed rapidly down the stairs to escape. They were almost at the door when they heard a voice.

"Great, you're here! Let's go."

Jeff, whose room was on the first floor, next to the stairway, had popped out of his room at the exact moment the two women had reached the door.

It was almost as if he'd planned it.

The three of them walked back to the Burton dormitory, Helen situated in the middle to preclude any presumptuous interdigitation from Jeff's wandering hands.

Once dropped off at the dorm, Jeff stopped by the front desk and managed to wrangle Pam's room number and phone number from the student working the desk.

So much for personal privacy rights.

●

Jeff had gone on a walking tour of Boston with another frat during rush week, so he thought a similar tour would be a great first date with Pam. He noticed the cross that Pam wore around her neck and was thus reasonably certain she wasn't going to attend the X-rated registration day movie.[*]

A plan was formulated.

"So, are you going to the registration day movie?" he asked soon after she answered his call, confident that her answer would allow him to cleverly substitute his alternate date plan.

Pam, however, was shocked (*shocked!*) that Jeff would even ask her such a thing. Did he really think she wanted to see an X-rated movie? Maybe she'd been right all along about these guys from the big city.

Jeff's plan was starting to backfire, big time. His credibility, along with his chances of ever seeing Pam a second time, were plummeting rapidly.

Backpedaling furiously, Jeff explained that he had no intention of seeing such a movie, either.

"I never meant to imply that I ever would see such a thing," he sputtered.

Accepting his explanatory utterances, Pam eventually relented and agreed to the walking tour.

On their way back, they stopped for a while at a bench overlooking the Charles River and talked. This became "their bench." Over the next four years, they spent many hours talking about life and love at this same spot.

In her junior year, Pam eventually joined WILG, living on the fourth floor, much closer to her sweetie than at Burton.

•

At Friday meals, brothers were allowed to bring guests. At the start of each meal, each brother with a guest stood up and introduced his guest. Pam, of course, had been to a great many of these meals and was well-known to everyone in the house.

On one such occasion in his senior year, Jeff stood up and

---

[*] Although it may be hard to imagine in today's environment, in the years surrounding our chapter's startup, the Lecture Series Committee (LSC), which organized full-campus lectures and movies throughout the semester, would show a XXX pornographic movie on registration day, with the full knowledge and silent approval of the MIT administration.

announced, "This is my fiancé, Pam Wolf." After a moment of comprehension, much congratulatory finger-snapping ensued.

Their wedding was planned for the day before graduation, a date when the couple figured nearly everyone would either still be in town or would be coming for the graduation ceremony.

Planning for the wedding kept Jeff busy enough that he had to skip the fraternity's newly-started annual tradition of an end-of-year Cape Cod retreat.

Amid the rush of planning activities, he got a letter from the MIT registrar informing him that he hadn't met graduation requirements. Several required courses were missing.

A few frenzied calls revealed the fact that the signed paperwork, detailing acceptable substitute courses, had been sitting on Jeff's advisor's desk for nearly two years.

"I'll bring it right over to the registrar's office," his advisor promised.

"I'll be calling them in an hour," Jeff assured him.

Don't make me come over there!

And it was finally resolved.

Had the wedding not been set for that particular date, Jeff would have been out at the Cape Cod retreat with the frat, and he wouldn't have gotten the letter until it was too late to graduate.

And that was how Jeff and Pam's marriage allowed Jeff to graduate from MIT.

He owes her big time.

•

From meeting at our very first fraternity party, through college dating years, to marriage and graduation on consecutive days, to a life shared, Pam and Jeff are the earliest ADP/WILG success story, dating back to the first week of our chapter's existence.

They've traveled around the world together as Jeff was employed at Hewlett Packard, so much so that each of their four children was born in a different country.

They've certainly come a long way since Pam tried to escape from this "big city" boy.

Tony Pelham

Nowadays, she even lets him hold her hand.

Pam Wolf and Jeff Thiemann

September 1976

MIT News:

> Hewlett-Packard, Texas Instruments and National Semiconductor(!) calculator ads flood the pages of The Tech. National offers a reverse Polish notation calculator for the unheard-of price of $25!

World and Local News:

> "The Muppet Show" premieres on television. President Ford and challenger Jimmy Carter prepare to square off for their first debate. Two old guys in the balcony seats prepare to heckle them. Carter's blockbuster interview with Playboy magazine is released, where he confesses to committing "lust in his heart."

•

Alferd D. Peters makes his first appearance at the frat. Andy Bronstein tapes or impales a huge cockroach on the bulletin board on the first-floor stairway landing. According to Andy, the spelling was a nod to Alferd Packer, the "Colorado Cannibal" who was buried in Andy's hometown.

Alferd soon begins to receive mail at the house address. The name of Alferd D. Peters eventually became attached to all house business accounts, including the telephone line.

•

Andy cooks a meatloaf dinner. The recipe calls for adding eggs to the hamburger to allow it to be properly shaped. Andy is not entirely clear on how this will help the shaping process, but he diligently buries half a dozen hard-boiled eggs into the loaves.

At dinner, diners are amazed and amused at discovering oval white and yellow egg sections embedded in their slices. Today, trendy New York restaurants charge forty dollars a plate for such innovation.

Andy's meals frequently involve the use of food coloring in new, exciting, and often unappetizing, ways. Never one to overlook the importance of symbolism, Andy used fire extinguishers as table centerpieces to celebrate "fiery" taco night.

As long as Andy didn't add Alferd D. Peters to his recipes, we were generally okay.

•

Corky Corcoran teaches Adrian to drive the stick shift on his VW Beetle. His transmission was never the same.

•

The Lambda Phi chapter of the Inebriation Foundation is officially founded.

A hole is drilled in one of the surplus apartment refrigerators in the basement, and a beer tap is installed to repurpose it into a "kegerator."

The Inebriation Foundation is entirely self-funded. A high-tech recording device—aka a piece of paper—is taped to the front where members mark each time a beer is consumed to make sure funds are available to purchase the next keg.

Members gain a quick understanding of "drunk" costs.

•

ADP fields its first intramural team— "C"-League soccer, and records a 1-0 victory against Phi Sigma Kappa. As only half of our team has ever played soccer before, the victory appears to be a minor miracle.

However, an asterisk in "The Tech" reveals the victory was a forfeit. Team captain Bob Glatz gives the team an inspirational speech. "We'll take a win any way we can get it. Who's going to Fathers?" *

●

Our supply of rapidly deteriorating pre-owned furniture is supplemented with a more modern, modular style that is delivered to the house regularly. This new line of furniture can be assembled and disassembled in seconds for placement whenever and wherever needed.

Best of all, the furniture costs nothing, making the treasurer and house manager extremely happy.

---

* "Father's" was shorthand for "Father's Fore," the bar across the street about a block away. It was part of a franchise of "Father's" bars in the Boston area: Father's First, Father's Too, Fathers Three, Father's Fore, and Father's Five.

Matt Alves enjoys a nutritious breakfast while seated on our modular furniture. Loren Kohnfelder and Russ Kalis are in the back.

•

We use empty "number 10" cans to collect leftover grease from cooking. One can is quickly filled to the brim. A piece of cloth is fashioned as a wick, and the resultant 'can'dle is placed in the air shaft between the apartment kitchen and the building next door.

With great solemnity, the wick is lighted. Lambda Phi's

'eternal flame' is born.
It burns brightly for months.

October 1976

MIT News:

A twelve-page ad in The Tech touts the upcoming Hifi Show sponsored by Tech Hifi. Stereo systems range from $200-$650 ($900-$3,000!). Tech Hifi was started in the 60s by two MIT students with their first location on Mass Ave, a few blocks from the frat, near the railroad tracks. Already at 48 locations, they would grow to reach 80. A true success story. In ten years, they will be out of business.

World and Local News:

President Gerald Ford declares in his second televised debate with Jimmy Carter that "there is no Soviet domination of Eastern Europe." Whoops!

MIT is not the only local school with dorm overcrowding problems. Wellesley College has so many extra students that 23 are housed in a portion of their infirmary. At least these students are in the right place if they get homesick.

•

Our fraternity dinners slowly start to stabilize. Misfires are happening less frequently. Cooking teams are beginning to be able to prepare some meals semi-independently. We invite guests on Fridays with some degree of confidence that they will not gag on our food.

On one memorable evening, I schedule "Knox Blox" for dessert. Knox Blox were an attempt by the Knox Gelatin Company to make inroads into industry leader Jello's market share by coming up with a "double-strength" recipe that made the resulting jello cubes firm enough to be picked up and eaten as finger food.

The colorful cubes prove too tempting to our testosterone-toting tools. One Blok flies across the room, smacking a shocked brother directly in the keister. A moment of stunned silence is followed by what seemed to be hundreds of Blox flying simultaneously in every direction. No person or surface in the basement dining room is spared from this Bloxness monster.

It's all over in a matter of seconds. The ammo is exhausted. There are no "seconds" on desserts.

The cleaning crew is irate.

I quietly cross off Knox Blox from my list of future dessert selections.

Knox Blox.

•

We lose to ZBT in C-League intramural soccer, 5-0. I am recruited to play, even though I am a D-leaguer on my best day. I'm a right-leg-only kicker.

On one memorable play, I kick the ball with full force at the exact instant a player from the other team kicks with the same force, in the opposite direction. It's a textbook physics lesson.

The ball remains motionless.

My knee ligaments do not. I'm out of the game, as I can no longer run. I can barely walk.

I visit the MIT infirmary for a checkup. The physician provides an astute assessment.

"Yep, looks like you hurt your knee."

Thanks, doc.

He advises RICE.*

That shouldn't be a problem, I think, as I'm the person in charge of menu planning.

Bob Glatz, our team captain, needs players for our next game. I agree to play goalie, the only soccer position one could conceivably play while not being able to run or kick. He gives me a five-minute goalie lesson on learning to dive for the ball.

"Dive, dive, dive."

For a minute, I think I'm on a WWII submarine. I practice diving on the soft dirt.

In the game, a shot comes. I don't dive. It's a goal. Five minutes of practice are not enough to overcome my natural inclination not to hurl my body onto the ground. Bob raises his hands in wonderment.

"Which part of dive did you not understand?"

On one occasion I actually stop the ball. I watch as everyone on both sides runs down the field. I'm supposed to kick the ball to the middle of the field, presumably to someone on our team. Only one problem. I can't kick with my bum knee. And I can't use my left leg. I'm a right-leg-only kicker.

"Stop! Come back!"

My shouts and arm waving are to no avail. Everyone just keeps running. This must be Bob's response to my perceived lack of effort.

Eventually, I just kick the ball, or maybe throw it, as far as I can. It goes only ten yards. The opposing team swarms back and fires in a shot on goal.

I don't dive.

---

* Rest, Ice, Compression, and Elevation.

This time, it's personal.

•

A group of brothers, including Rob Mandel and Andy Bronstein, frequent Baskin-Robbins ice cream in Central Square. Rob spots the watermelon ice, and asks the attendant:

"Are there seeds in the watermelon ice?"

"No."

"Well, you need to think about it. You could be eating it and spitting out the seeds. Can you ask corporate about the possibility?"

Obnoxiously, Rob does this same spiel on at least three occasions.

Before their next visit, Andy collects a container full of watermelon seeds. Shortly before the group goes again, Andy brings the seeds to the shop and convinces the attendant to mix the seeds into a single serving of watermelon ice.

Shortly after, the gang arrives.

Rob launches into his familiar routine.

"Are there seeds in the watermelon ice?"

The attendant is ready.

"Yes, there are!"

She whips out a cone, complete with genuine watermelon seeds.

Rob, initially astonished, accepts the pre-seeded cone with great wonderment and awe. He happily spits out the seeds as the group walks back to the frat, all the while stating that he's never going back to that "seedy" ice cream shop.

Statues With No Limitations

Corky Corcoran awoke to find his car missing.

You gotta be fucking kidding me!

Big cities, like the Boston/Cambridge area, were notorious car theft capitals. This couldn't be happening to him. Not now.

Maybe I parked it in a different place.

What had he been doing last night? It was all a haze. A few dim memories began to drift back.

He was out drinking, with five chapter members. They had had quite a few pitchers...

A thought suddenly came to his mind. He reached into his pocket.

Aww, shit!

•

"It's all about prestige," Corky had explained to the group that surrounded him.

"The top chapters, the ones with the most spirit—they're the only ones who do it."

The message made an impression on a few of the pledges. Others, like myself, thought it was a vaguely entertaining notion, but the idea of actually driving over to another chapter for a 'heist' seemed a tad too much.

"If someone were to, hypothetically, want to obtain one of these statues, where would one get it?" Al asked, a little too obviously.

Corky knew the exact location of each statue in every ADP chapter.

"The closest is probably at Dartmouth, in Vermont," Corky responded. "Although that chapter's not even part of the International, anymore. Those cheap bastards didn't want to pay the dues. So now they just call themselves Alpha Delta. But they hung onto their statue. They've got it chained to the bottom of their main staircase."

"Not for long," freshman Carl Heinzl whispered to himself.

"How far away is Dartmouth?"

"About a two-hour drive," Corky replied.

To Carl, "the animal," that translated to about ninety minutes—if he were driving.

Now, where to get a car.

•

The heater lever in the Beetle seemed to exist for decorative purposes only. The five passengers shivered, and where they were headed, it was only going to get colder.

Al Mink, piloting the borrowed Bug, along with four darkly-clothed passengers, was not exactly cat burglar-like in stature. Al, Jeff Thiemann, and Matt Alves were among the tallest members of the chapter, each well over six feet, Carl Heinzl, solid and stocky, had more of a football build. Andy Bronstein was the only member who could have conceivably be thought of as stealthy.

The plan, at least so far, had worked to perfection. Get Corky drunk, and when he passed out in his room, extract his keys, and "borrow" his VW Beetle.

Mike Corcoran would contend, many years later, that he had been premeditatedly "plied" with alcohol. He would not be incorrect.

A trip to a hardware store in Central Square earlier in the day had yielded the requisite bolt-cutters that were going to be needed to 'liberate' the statute from the Dartmouth chapter house.

The five spent their time going over every possible scenario they could conjure up, and how they would respond.

When engineers plan a heist, no one can say that they don't have a plan—or in this case—many contingency plans.

The four-hour drive, round trip, together with the time needed to "extract" the statue from the Dartmouth chapter house, meant that they should be able to get back before Corky ever realized his car was gone.

Well, it was a nice thought.

•

The Brothers in Arms statue, almost always referred to as "Mike & Ike," is a memorial to members of Alpha Delta Phi, from the United States and Canada, who served in World War I, and especially to those who perished.

Mike and Ike, the two figures in the statue, represent a Canadian and an American officer who are helping each other through the battle. The statue is "featured prominently in Alpha Delt chapter houses across the country."

It was created by Captain Robert Aitken, the same artist who created the nine-figured sculpture in front of the Supreme Court Building in Washington, D.C. [21]

One copy of the Brothers in Arms sculpture even resided in the Smithsonian Art Museum.

In addition to the one that would hopefully soon be residing in our chapter house.

•

The group of five reached the Dartmouth chapter house well after midnight. Al parked the car a fair distance from the house, to avoid suspicion.

Initial reconnaissance indicated that the Dartmouth Alpha Delts had held a party earlier that evening.

---

[21] http://middletown.adps.org/about/mike-n-ike/

No big surprise, there.

As a consequence, the front door of the house was wide open. A decision had to be made. Sneak in—and be on the lookout for any Dartmouth brothers—or simply stride in boldly, like partygoers who were just a little bit late to the party, and who just so happened to be carrying a gigantic set of bolt cutters with them.

Hiding the bolt-cutters underneath clothing appeared to present unacceptable risks to one's manhood, particularly if one had to make a mad dash to escape.

The stealth entry option was selected.

With Al Mink manning the getaway vehicle, the four freshmen crept up to the chapter house. The first to enter heard voices from the upper floors and the basement pub, but no one was seen or heard on the first floor.

•

While waiting, Dartmouth campus patrol came by to check out why this green VW Beetle was parked on campus by the side of the road, with a lone occupant sitting behind the wheel.

"Just having some battery problems," Al explained to the officer. "I've got some people coming by to give me a push in a few minutes."

Al's fervent hope was that his "people" wouldn't come bolting around the corner at that exact moment, lugging a metal statue. That might be a little harder to explain.

•

The statue was chained at the base of the stairway, within a few feet of the front door, just as Corky had described.

One man steadied the statue. Jeff readied himself to remove the chains from the bolt and from around the statue after the bolt cutters had worked their magic. A third person remained as a lookout.

The fourth, accomplished cat-burglar Andy Bronstein, carefully worked the cutter's blades around the bolt's shackle and squeezed the handles together.

A sharp crack echoed throughout the house.

They had anticipated that the noise would alert the brothers, so chains were hurriedly removed, and Jeff and one other person hoisted the statue from the pedestal, and the four thieves raced to the waiting car.

Fortunately, the statue fit within the small front trunk of the Beetle. Not so fortunately, the hood didn't close all the way.

Carl quickly resolved the issue by sitting on top of the car's hood during the initial getaway, until they had cleared the campus, after which a repositioning of the statue allowed the hood to close, and Carl to avoid frostbite of his nether regions.

•

Corky waited impatiently for the crew to return, as they eventually did, later that morning. Prepared to give them a hard time for their "appropriation" of his desperately needed means of transportation, his countenance quickly reversed upon seeing Mike & Ike being extracted from his trunk.

He only had one question for the five men.

Did you remember to put gas in the car?

Mike later related that he was "never prouder" than when he saw these men first return with the statue.

Along with his only means of transportation, of course.

Jeff recalls that it took all five of them to hoist the trophy out of the VW's trunk. It seemed to weigh at least twice as much as when the two of them had grabbed it from the Dartmouth chapter and taken off running.

A little adrenaline will do that, boys.

•

A month or so later, someone in the MIT administration relayed a request to one of our officers.

That statue that you 'don't have,' really 'don't have' it a week from now.

The Dartmouth Alpha Delts had gone through university channels—as in President of Dartmouth to President of MIT— to put pressure on us to return the statue.

MIT campus patrol also came by to inform us that this act

would constitute a felony unless it was returned immediately, and that crossing state lines with stolen goods bumped this up to a federal offense.

It wasn't hard to figure out how Dartmouth knew it was us that did the deed.

Corky wouldn't have been above calling up a certain chapter who had withdrawn from the national fraternity, to rub it in their faces that a certain other chapter just might have their statue.

It's also certain that no one anticipated Dartmouth's threatening response over some 'friendly' college hijinks.

According to Andy, we had never intended to keep Dartmouth's Mike & Ike. Our escapade was just to show that we could get it whenever we wanted to. It was all in the name of good-natured fraternity rivalry.

Until the Institute got involved.

A subsequent trip was instigated. The statue was stealthily returned to its original plinth at Dartmouth along with a six-pack of beer—a token of appreciation for the 'loan.' No contact was made with the Dartmouth chapter members, just in case.

Thanks, bros!

•

For some time, Mike & Ike statues were stolen by various chapters, including ours. The International generally frowned on this, in part, because the statue is meant as a memorial to our fallen dead and was not considered to be part of a prank.

As a replacement, the "Henry P. Havlik Traveling Trophy" was created. This trophy was designed to be stolen. There were rules: it must not be bolted down, and it must be displayed in a prominent, accessible location in the chapter.

But nowhere did it say anything about an alarm system.

November 1976

MIT News:

> The Tech reports on MIT dorm food costs. The full plan (19 meals/week) runs $565 ($2,600) per term. The article also discusses fraternity food plans, contrasting those where brothers cook against plans with paid chefs, noting that it's the difference *"between eating the meals cooked by an experienced professional or by a brother who may be majoring in chemical engineering or vivisection."*

World and Local News:

> Jimmy Carter is elected as the 39th President of the United States. The election, however, begins the process of coalescing many religious groups to support future Republican candidates. Politics in this country will never be the same

•

There is some, possibly heated, discussion regarding the treatment of the two pledge classes. Should all twenty-two be part of a single pledge class, or is there a distinction between the first ten and the second group of twelve?

Tom Burgmann recalls that a decision was made from "on high," i.e., from the ADP International Board. The first group of ten would be initiated together in the first semester. The second group of twelve would be initiated in the second semester.

He was not pleased, as he felt this went against the message about "building a new fraternity together" that was stressed during rush week.

The decision thus made, the second group of twelve comes up with their identity—the 'Dirty Dozen,' to distinguish themselves, given their new, decidedly second-tier, status.

With no name for the first pledge class, members of the Dirty Dozen begin referring to their predecessors, somewhat sarcastically, as the 'original ten.'

The name sticks, as the first group concludes, correctly, that the sarcastic nature of the name would eventually be forgotten. [*]

And the name has a nice "superhero" vibe going for it.

•

A group of alumni, including David Eddy and Paul Stewart, completes work on the house in preparation for the initiation ceremony.

The Original Ten pledge class receives only minimal pledge training. Jon Cohen recalls that we had to memorize several songs, including ADP and MIT songs.

It was only years later that Al realized his knowledge of ADP and LP history, lore, and songs was far more limited than most of the succeeding pledge classes.

We did, however, know quite a bit about the Original Ten.

My knowledge at this point can be succinctly summed up as Samuel Eells, Alpha Delta Phi, something, something, something, and Henry Leeb, Lambda Phi, blah, blah, blah.

Though I did know about Lambda Phi alumnus Mortimer Budlong, from firsthand experience.

Jon Cohen is our star, the only pledge of the original ten who knows every verse of our songs. Truly, he outshines us all by far.

Initiation day, Saturday, November 13, finally arrives. This is also the day the new Chapter is installed. Various Alpha Delts from other chapters arrive at the house to conduct the

---

[*] Until this writing.

proceedings.

Bob Wolf recalls that the members of the Dirty Dozen pledge class were required to remain in their rooms while the initiation activities were going on.

Hopefully, we let them use the bathrooms.

Specific details of the initiation itself are, of course, secret. After the ceremony, the "Original Ten" pledge class finally become honest men. We were legit. A fantastic banquet followed, attended by most of the Alpha Delts who had provided so much support for our startup: Andrew Onderdonk, Bob McKelvey, Bob Price, David Eddy, and Paul Stewart.

We were, and continue to be, extremely grateful to these men for their spirit of generosity and brotherhood.

•

I check in on the Tuesday cooking crew as they prepare dinner. Rob Mandel is preparing the salad. Bent over, back towards me, he's engrossed in his work. I can see he's holding a paring knife.

What the hell is he doing to the salad?

"Hey, Moose, how's it going?" I ask, finally getting his attention.

Rob performs a last cut with the knife. He turns and holds up his masterpiece for my inspection.

It's a perfectly circumcised cucumber.

This was not what I had expected to see. I'm a little taken aback.

Rob is thrilled at my reaction.

"They serve these for lunch at Wang Labs," he quips, punning on the name of a prominent computer firm at the time.

"Are you just going to throw that in the salad?" I ask, not knowing what to expect as an answer.

"Of course not. I'll slice it first."

"What about the end?"

He slices off the tip, pops it in his mouth, chews, and swallows.

"Problem solved!"

He beams.

Years later, while in med school, Rob is put on a pediatric rotation. In his role, he performs circumcisions on real live infants, although these only have baby gherkins.

Rob's fraternity cooking experience has prepared him well for his future career in medicine.

Thank goodness he didn't go into gynecology.

•

Beer chugging competitions have become one of our most popular extra-curricular activities, sponsored, in part, by the Inebriation Foundation.

Two four-person teams line up facing each other. Starting from one end, each person on each team must finish their pint before the next person starts, then the order reverses.

This means that the fourth person, the "anchor," must drink two pints in a row. Carl Heinzl is always, always, the anchor. And Carl's teams always, always, win.

Occasionally, WILG fields a team to compete against us. We are impressed just that they are willing to try.

WILG even has their own "Carl Heinzl" to anchor its team.

We are even more impressed.

WILG's anchor credits her prowess to the fact that she doesn't like the taste of beer, so she downs it as fast as is humanly possible.

That will work.

Carl challenges Bob Glatz to see who can chug the fastest. Bob Glatz is no slouch when it comes to beer-drinking, but he knows he has zero chance to win against a legend. He refuses the challenge.

Carl ups the ante. "I'll chug a pitcher. You chug a pint."

There's no way Carl can down a whole pitcher before Bob can drink a pint. Bob accepts, confident that, for once in his life, he's going to beat Carl at his own game.

The signal is given, and Bob tilts his mug. Down to his last few ounces, he begins preparing his victory speech. At that moment, he hears an unmistakable sound.

The "thunk" of Carl's pitcher on the table.

This is immediately followed by a tremendous belch that shakes the entire room.

Once again, Carl has accomplished the impossible. And Bob has learned a valuable lesson.

You can never outdrink an "animal."

Figure 1 – Carl "The Animal" Heinzl, Rob Mandel, Louis Cohen, and Jeff Thiemann strike serious poses outside of Spanky's, directly across the street.

December 1976

MIT News:

> A Computer Mart ad in The Tech touts microcomputer kits and fully assembled systems, including Z-80 and Southwest Technical Products systems. Their ad provides instructions for the two different busses required to get to their Waltham store from Harvard Square. It will be years before such systems standardize on a single bus.

World and Local News:

> John Disher, NASA's Director of Advanced Programs, states that "eventually, I am sure that we are going to be using solar energy from space here on Earth." Other long-range plans include electronic mail transfer via space satellites and the use of space as a reservoir for Earth's waste products.

•

The never-ending duties of the food steward, in addition to other aspects of my life, are taking their toll on me. At the time, I have a serious relationship, I am playing on the squash team, and I am involved in activities at a local church. My first semester of classes with grades is not going well.

I am reluctant to give up any of my 'extra-curricular' activities. All of them are important to my life. But people in the frat need to eat.

I am constantly exhausted and eventually resort to taking caffeine pills to stay awake in classes. My college experience is turning into a nightmare. I am having second—and third— thoughts about fraternity life.

I perform inexplicably poorly on tests and exams. My digital electronics lab project—almost my entire grade in the class—is turning into a disaster. As I had only signed up for four classes, I don't feel that I can drop the class. I have to stick it out.

In hindsight, it was clear I had too much on my plate. My poor academic performance was due in a large part to fatigue and anxiety from lack of sleep.

The elections for second-term officers are here. This is my chance. I explain I need help with the food steward job. I can't keep up with it. It's way too much work for one person, and it's never-ending.

I'm not sure how I am convinced to stay in the position for the second semester, but the food steward position is expanded to include two assistant food stewards. Bret Hartman and Chris King fill the spots.

My life begins to get better, even just with the thought of getting some relief.

As it turns out, both Chris and Bret are extremely capable and handle the lion's share of the work going forward.

I can finally begin to breathe.

•

The dessert looked promising, but to the keen observer, perhaps a tad bit suspicious. The whipped cream filled the pie crust completely, showing no other ingredients. Where had we seen this before?

And why is there only one pie for twenty-two people? Things aren't adding up.

Bob Wolf, the pledge trainer for the Dirty Dozen pledge class, had noticed a bit of an attitude cropping up among certain pledges. Maybe it was the fact that they resented not being initiated along with the Original Ten. Or maybe they just needed to assert some degree of autonomy after being relegated to second-tier status.

Bob Glatz decides to show the pledges' autonomy the old-fashioned way. With a pie in the face. Almost all the pledges know what was about to take place.

Bob Wolf never sees it coming. Some of the brothers notice what is about to go down, but interestingly, no one intervenes. They want to see how this whole thing plays out.

And it plays to perfection. Surprise. Shock. Bewilderment. Realization. Bob Wolf wiping whipped cream off his face, totally flustered.

Bob runs out of the basement dining room, up the stairs, only to find David Eddy at the front entrance, knocking at the door.

Bob opens the door for David, who takes one look at him and comments:

"Well, I guess things haven't changed that much."

•

The elections see us elect quite a few members of the next pledge class to house offices. Tom Burgmann and Loren Kohnfelder discuss whether each should run for the office of president during the second term. Tom eventually decides his busy social life with Fern Crandall takes precedent over being president, leaving Loren to run unopposed.

Adrian passes the torch to Loren as the new president. Al Mink remains as vice-president to provide continued support and assistance from that role.

Members of the new pledge class take on house offices of pledge trainer, secretary, social chair, and house critic, in addition to the two new assistant food stewards.

Next year, after the constitution is passed, only initiated brothers will be allowed to hold these offices.

The torch is being passed. The initial era, from April to December, where only the Original Ten are running the show, is coming to an end.

There's a new gang in town.

January 1977

MIT News:

An editorial in *The Tech* opines about the proper name of the MIT athletic teams. Currently, various MIT teams employ three different names. Some are Beavers, some are Engineers, and some are Techmen. The editorial writer favors Beavers.

The Women's swim team raises money by selling t-shirts emblazoned with "Nothing beats a wet beaver!" They quickly sell out, showing a surprising degree of male support for the team.

World and Local News:

Jimmy Carter is sworn in as the 39th President on January 20th. One day later he issues a pardon to Vietnam War draft evaders.

•

In between semesters, life has taken on a more relaxed air for the house members who stay in January. No meals are prepared. It's every man for himself.

We have many gallons of extra milk left over after the semester ended. For some unknown reason, demand drops precipitously with almost everyone gone. Most likely I had forgotten to cancel, or at least reduce, our standing milk order before the Christmas break. The extra milk turns sour.

Jon Cohen discovers that sour milk is potable, and even enjoyable if approached with the correct attitude. It is not clear if this has anything to do with his being treasurer.

His lactococcal evangelization fails to gain any other converts, however. Impressively, working alone, he makes a substantial dent in the overage over the course of the month.

That's money in the bank, right there.

•

A second Alferd D. Peters appears, now taking the form of Andy's pet white rat. This Alferd prospers and makes various appearances throughout the semester for educational and entertainment purposes. Andy maintains that Alferd eventually reached a weight greater than four and a half pounds, much of it attributed to Alferd's lifelong membership in the Inebriation Foundation.

Notably, however, it was not Alferd's noggin that later surfaced in the form of a "head" of beer.

Not Alferd's head of beer

•

A new recreational activity takes over the chapter house. Water fights. Every manner of advanced water pistol, gun, and weapon is utilized in long-running, multi-floor water battles. As our building is due to be completely renovated, not much concern is given about the effects of the drenching on the building's interior.

It's a free-for-all.

The escalating arms race of water weaponry continues until one brother or pledge unveils the ultimate water weapon—the so-called "moriah." A long length of latex surgical tubing, when filled from a faucet, it becomes a water-filled snake-like balloon capable of holding up to ten gallons of water.

A filled moriah, weighing some eighty pounds, is looped around the carrier's body, its substantial weight supported on one shoulder. It's capable of projecting a stream of water up to twenty-five feet in one continuous shot for minutes.

The water wars are over. All hail the Moriah.

Moriah's, and all other large water projecting devices, will be banned the next year in our newly renovated building.

•

Al Mink drives his VW beetle to the house from Florida. The engine needs repairs. He manages to remove the engine and bring it into the basement for work.

The rest of the car is left out in the rear of the chapter house. The next time Al checks, the car has disappeared. With no engine, he figures it can't have gone too far.

A team of brothers fans out and finds the car down the block, stripped.

Al's Bug has been zapped.

With a bad engine and stripped body, the car is a total loss.

The VW flat-four engine still has intrinsic value, however. It is a large, heavy object weighing on the order of 200-250 pounds, large enough to make a delightful impact with the ground, at approximately 56 ft/second, after a drop from a height of 50 feet or so.

It's not so large that it cannot be carried up the stairs by four strapping lads, which is exactly what happens, followed by a real-life recreation of Newton's gravitational thought experiment regarding falling objects.

Newton is vindicated, once again. And the flat-four engine becomes an even-flatter four.

Engine drop

February 1977

MIT News:

> The annual "Tuition riot" is held on February 2. Traffic is blocked on all but
> one lane of Mass Ave. Additionally, students throw snowballs at the newly
> installed Transparent Horizon statue, selected as symbolic of the institute's
> "wasteful" spending. They shout "Forty-three fifty, too damn much!" to
> protest the newly announced eight percent tuition increase to $4350.

World and Local News:

> The space shuttle *Enterprise* goes on its first "flight," atop a Boeing 747, at
> Edwards Air Force Base in California. Constructed with no engines or
> functional heat shield, Enterprise was never refitted for orbital flight but was
> used extensively to test various aspects of the shuttle system, including pilot-
> controlled landings.

•

At every house meeting, the phrase "next year, when the
renovation is done..." is heard more and more often in many
house officer's reports.

"Next year, when the renovation is done, we'll have space for
parties."

"...we'll have a living room for these meetings."

"...we'll have a commercial kitchen."

"...we'll have a real dining room."

"...we'll have an outdoor deck."

It's becoming clear we are living for the future. And speaking of the future, we begin to formulate plans for the next year's rush and try to determine how many pledges to target. Our new facility will have space for nearly sixty, but it's clear that pledging thirty or more new members is not feasible or desirable.

Still, MIT will be upping the rent next year as we begin to occupy 55% of the building. We need to at least double our size. But the slow fraternity rush the previous year means that almost all fraternities will be looking for more new members than usual. Rushing twenty-two or more freshmen, double the average for other fraternities, will be a formidable challenge.

•

Pledge training for the "Dirty Dozen" pledge class is wrapping up. Bob Glatz takes over from Bob Wolf after the first semester, continuing in our tradition of having pledge classes train themselves.*

The transition was perhaps due, in part, to the earlier pie-in-the-face incident in which Bob Wolf may have gotten a tad fed up with these young upstarts.

You think you're so smart? Okay, train yourselves.

The International Board of Directors is not happy that a pledge is *once again* training pledges. For the first pledge class, it was unavoidable. The second time was on us.

We duly note their concerns and promptly ignore them.

Who says MIT hasn't taught us anything?

The "Dirty Dozen" pledge class has to master considerably more material than we did, but it will not compare to what is coming in the future.

•

---

* This will not be possible when the constitution is passed next year, forbidding pledges from holding this office.

The initiation for our second pledge class is held, just two months after the first pledge class.

By this time, all original Lambda Phis have been inducted into Alpha Delta Phi, some posthumously. All living LPs are invited to the initiation ceremony and banquet, and nine attend the ceremony, including Mortimer Budlong.

We now have twenty-two brothers in the house.

We are definitely off the ground.

•

My girlfriend, Michele, volunteers to make dessert for our Friday dinner, where brothers can bring dates. She bakes "hermit cakes," a family specialty, which are small, sweet molasses cookie/muffin concoctions.

She bakes enough for all the brothers and guests. It takes her a good portion of the day to cook enough to supply the needs of our "many." Like many of our first-time cooks, she is at first overwhelmed by the sheer quantities involved in preparing meals for so many people.

And that's just dessert!

Dinner is done. Her dessert is served. Each table receives its allotted number of cakes. Something is vaguely disquieting about the cakes, but I can't quite put my finger on it. They're rectangular and perfectly palm-sized. They have a nice "heft" to them.

My eyes widen. I look over and see Carl "the animal" Heinzl with a peculiar grin on his face.

"No, Carl, no!"

It's too late.

It happens again.

Hermit cakes fly across the room as the room transitions into a flurry of heat-seeking molasses missiles.

Like our previous food fight, it's over almost before it starts. Crumbs and pieces of hermit cakes litter the floor. At least they don't splatter and stick to the walls like Knox Blox.

Be thankful for small blessings.

Michele is horrified. Nothing in her experience prepared her for this. Her hours of cooking effort are wasted. I resist the temptation to tell her that her effort hadn't been wasted, it was just repurposed into a form that she hadn't originally anticipated.

Fortunately, I managed to hold onto my hermit cake. I offer her half. She remains motionless, saying nothing.

I get "the look."

Carl comes over, sensing that she may be upset. He attempts to placate her by stating that he took a bite of one, before initiating the frenzy.

"They were good."

Carl gets "the look."

He backs away, slowly.

Michele will never, ever, prepare anything for the frat again.

March 1977

MIT News:

> The Institute's Mass Ave crossing signal is hacked from 'Walk/Don't Walk' to 'Walk/Chew.' In other news, hundreds of gum-snapping MIT students are run over while attempting to cross the street.

> Jockey advertises in The Tech, promoting "dual-purpose underwear," designed to be "both underwear and everything from swimwear to gym clothes and walking shorts." Thanks to Jockey, "wearing your underwear on the outside is going to be very, very, 'in.' " Umm, that would be a no.

World News:

> The infrared telescope fitted on the Kuiper Airborne Observatory discovers evidence for rings around the planet Uranus, leading to the unforgettable headline in the Boston Globe on March 16, "Is there a ring of debris around... Uranus?"

•

One of the members of WILG gets a pet. A kitten. The kitten seems to have free reign of the house and wanders up and down the stairs and enters peoples' rooms—sometimes without even knocking.

I'm up very early one morning, as per my routine, working at my desk. The kitten, keenly sensing signs of life anywhere in the building, seeks me out. It hops up on my ancient army surplus desk to provide moral support as I tackle my latest problem set.

It spots my mug containing the last remnants of my morning tea. Curiosity overwhelms it. It dips its tiny paw into the mug to "test the waters."

It's wet!

Kittens apparently don't like wet paws. Rapidly withdrawing its now dripping appendage, it shakes it vigorously, showering my face, my problem set, and the entire area with fine droplets of cold tea.

I'm fully awake now. Thank you.

Nonetheless, I like the kitten. It's cute and very friendly.

Not everyone, however, is fond of the cute fuzzball. Some people think that it should remain confined to WILG floors. As the kitten grows into a cat, it develops the unfortunate habit of leaving "daily deposits" outside of Andy's door.

After spending the day on campus, I return to the chapter house in the afternoon. I spot the cat walking down the stairs.

"Something's different," I note, astutely.

The cat sports a large green marking.

For St. Patrick's Day, Andy Bronstein has tagged the cat with a green mark, much in the same manner as sheep are marked in the field.

I hear shouting from upstairs. There's a tremendous commotion.

The cat's owner is not pleased.

She is raging, screaming, mad. Her face is beet red.

Andy counters her rage in his characteristic, laid-back style.

"You see what happens when you let your cat run free? Anyway, it's just food coloring. It'll wash out."

She is not mollified by Andy's explanations. Relations with WILG will take a turn for the worse.

The cat never comes down to see me again.

Happy St. Patrick's Day!

●

Andy "discovers" an orphaned toilet during one of his periodic forays in the excavated center section of the building. Of course, in our chapter, this can only mean one thing.

It must be thrown off the roof.

Part of the appeal is that a falling toilet problem has appeared in one of his Physics problem sets. Thus, his efforts fall under the category of empirical verification.

He corrals Matt Alves and Rob Mandel, and the three of them carry the toilet to the rear stairway of our occupied section, where they begin their ascent to the roof.

Along the way, they encounter one of the members of the women's group.

"What are you doing?" she asks.

"We are carrying this toilet up to the roof in order to throw it off."

"Oh."

It's not clear what answer would have caused her to intervene in any way, but this was not one of them.

Carry on, then.

The first throw landed on a pile of loose debris, which absorbed most of the shock of impact. To the dismay of the toilet tossing trio, the toilet survived, nearly intact.

There was only one course of action that reasonable people facing this situation must take.

We have to throw it again.

The second attempt hits at the intersection of concrete and

brick wall. The toilet explodes.

Much satisfaction is experienced from above.

Afterward, Rob Mandel spends significant time in self-reflection. He's just turned twenty. His role in the toilet affair has prompted deep, piercing, questions.

"I'm twenty years old for god's sakes. Is this the sign of a mature individual? Is this really what I want to be doing with my life? "

Rob will never throw another toilet off a roof, again.

Shafted

In the middle of the night, all door buzzers in all the rooms of the chapter house sound simultaneously.

Jolted awake, groggy brothers try to figure out what's happening. Then it hits them.

This is Jon's fault!

It had been a few weeks since the Henry P. Havlik Traveling Trophy had arrived at the house, the result of yet another nighttime appropriation from a nearby Alpha Delt chapter. As dictated by the rules, the trophy is prominently displayed, set on the mantle in our first-floor living room.

And Jon Cohen had had a brainstorm. The old apartment building had a "buzzer" entrance system, still semi-functional in the first year.

If he fastened a switch to the bottom of the trophy, he could rewire the old apartment buzzer entrance system so that all the buzzers would go off whenever the trophy was picked up.

In their sleepy stupor, awakened brothers initially figure this is some malfunction with Jon's 'stupid' alarm system, occurring at the worst time possible, when they are trying to sleep after a late weekend night.

But, what if...?

Brothers race to the living room lounge where the traveling trophy is displayed.

•

The two interlopers are not prepared for the sound of fifteen apartment buzzers permeating every cubic inch of the building at the very instant that they lift the trophy from the mantle.

They panic.

The front door to the frat is just down the hall. In just a few seconds, they could be out the door with their booty. Perhaps they think that the sounds of the buzzers have led brothers to immediately block the entranceway.

Instead, they decide to escape via one of the three windows in the room where they stand. There appears to be a source of light out that way.

The first man opens the window and climbs out.

"Quick, pass me the trophy."

Trophy successfully transferred, the second thief follows the first out into the night. Outside, the two look about in every direction.

Where the heck are we?

It is as if they'd entered another dimension. The walls of this narrow space appear to be closing in on them, with no discernable exit from the hellish brick cave they find themselves in. The air is fetid and foul as if no living creature had ventured into this abyss for an eternity.

Something catches their eye. To their left, they finally see the source of light that had led them into this place.

It is a large number ten commercial food can, with a flame burning brightly from the wick in its center.

It smells like bacon.

•

"They're in the air shaft!"

The adrenaline-infused brothers converge simultaneously

into the living room, where the sight before them turns thoughts of impending action into deep, soul-satisfying, amusement.

The two would-be thieves, holding the traveling trophy, stare at them from outside the living room window.

The thieves' unhappiness at their current state of affairs is more than offset by Jon Cohen's jubilation.

"It worked!" he says, almost as if he can't believe it.

"It worked!" comes the rejoinder from many other brothers, followed by a multitude of vigorous pats on the back.

Science, technology, and planning, coupled with a little bit of luck, have successfully prevented the trophy's appropriation.

The brothers allow the aspiring burglars back into the living room—only after they pass the trophy in first.

With the trophy back on the mantle, the buzzers mercifully go silent.

After introductions all around, they are escorted out of the building, this time via the front door. No hard feelings.

Better luck next time!

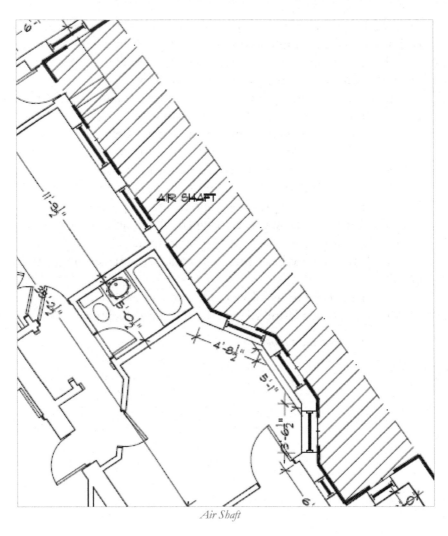

Air Shaft

Our chapter steals the traveling trophy so many times that we decide to personalize it. A metal sheep, taken from a 4-H trophy, is cemented on top, representing 'Lamb'da Phi.

Henry P. Havlik Traveling Trophy

April 1977

MIT News:

> A revolutionary new feature, the Automated Teller Machine, makes its way into various Cambridge banks near the fraternity. The ATM allows users to avoid waiting in long teller lines inside the bank. Instead, they wait in long ATM lines outside the bank, in the bitter cold.

> In the "Tennis Game of the Century," 1970 Nobel laureate MIT professor Paul Samuelson defeats (future) 1981 Nobel laureate Yale Professor James Tobin in the Irving Fisher All-Star Tennis Tournament, in a match officiated by (future) 1987 Nobel laureate Robert Solow. Solow comments that he "thinks the win vindicates our whole approach to teaching economics. The MIT precept of a sound mind in a healthy body has once again triumphed over whatever they do at Yale."

World and Local News:

> The Apple II computer, with color graphics display, is released. It sells well from its initial launch. Sales double every four months, growing from less than one million dollars annually to $118 million in 1980.

•

Adrian Zuckerman stares intently at the message on the green screen.

Insufficient funds. Card retained. See teller inside.

For the third time in less than a year, the ATM has "eaten" his card.

A poor college student with a perilously small, occasionally positive, checking account balance, Adrian, is pissed.

IHTFP. [*]

The next day, during "normal banking hours," i.e., between 9 am and 2 pm, Adrian takes time out from his schedule to physically enter the bank's lobby and make the "walk of shame," waiting in line for a teller and asking, maybe even begging, to have his card returned.

"Someday," he thinks as he waits, "I'm going to have enough money where I can take twenty goddamn dollars out of my goddamn checking account without worrying whether the fucking machine's going to eat my card."

Some people dream big.

•

The building renovation moves along swiftly. The Institute has a hard deadline for finishing the work. The entire building must be completed before September. Missing the deadline will mean the new living groups will not be able to occupy the house in time for the semester.

Worse yet, it would mean that the groups will not be able to conduct their rushes. And that would be a disaster for the already overcrowded housing system. The Institute massively front-loads the project.

The opposite side of the building, at 355 Mass Ave, is completed. Construction workers have nearly completed tearing down the upper four floors of the building's center rear section.

Renovation of the center's front section, containing the two groups' living and dining rooms, occurs concurrently with demolition.

All work on the center section needs to be finished before the summer, when the last third of the building needs to be absolutely, positively, ready for occupation by the end of August.

---

[*] I hate this place.

The building's unique layout provided a massive challenge for the demolition crew. There is not enough room for a swinging wrecking ball to smash existing stories, and the use of explosives is out of the question due to the section's proximity to the other rear building sections, not to mention to the church and other buildings behind the structure.

And they must keep bricks and other debris from falling outside the center section's footprint, as any loose, falling bricks could easily go through the windows of the adjacent sections, one section of which was currently occupied.

By us.

As a consequence, the team develops a unique demolition style. We watch, fascinated, as workers stand on top of each wall section, initially fifty feet above the pavement, and swing a sledgehammer at the brick wall directly underneath their feet. Swinging from the outside in, they must swing just hard enough to loosen the bricks to the point where they can be pulled in from the interior.

Swinging a little too aggressively and..., as they say, "that's all she wrote."

We wonder about the learning curve of such an endeavor. Our future mechanical and civil engineers argue about various alternative, superior, and presumably, safer approaches to this task.

If I was in charge...

But ultimately, MIT beckons, in the form of weekly problem sets, labs, and exam preparation. They leave the workers to their own devices.

Not really my problem.

Constructing the rear wall after upper floor demolition

The author with Jon Cohen, surveying the progress of the renovation

•

Our D-league intra-mural softball team plays our arch-rivals, the MIT Shakespeare Ensemble, aka the "Knaves." At one point, a line drive is hit down the third-base line. The two teams disagree on whether the ball landed in play or not. The call could go either way. Back and forth arguments ensue.

Team captain and house athletic chairman Rob Mandel seizes the moment and loudly proclaims.

"Fair is foul, and foul is fair."

Most of the members of the Shakespeare ensemble are rightly impressed with Brother Mandel's quick wit. They give him a "theater clap." Not every member of their team is so conciliatory, however. Some are heard muttering that "The Lambdas doth protest too much."

Later in the game, I hit a hard liner into left field. As I bolt out of the batter's box, it appears I might be able to stretch it into a double, but it's not a given by any means. Rounding first base, only one thought runs through my head:

2B or not 2B?

Adrian, Russ, and Steve try to figure how to use this leather thingy

•

Bret and Chris, the two assistant food stewards, have tackled their new jobs with great gusto. They've added a new component to the job—kitchen cleanup inspection.

After the cleaning crew "finishes," the crew must contact one of the two stewards to validate their efforts. The floor, counters, and all pots, and pans must be clean. Dishes and silverware must be washed, dried, and put away.

No exceptions.

The cleaning crew each night groans and complains about the amount of rework required.

Well, if you did it right the first time, you wouldn't have to do it again.

Occasionally, one hears mumbled references to "Herr Hartman."

Everyone else not on cleanup duty is thrilled with the newly revitalized kitchen.

There is a limit as to how clean anyone can get our old apartment kitchen. Bret and Chris are aware of this and don't expect perfection.

This will not be the case with the brand-new commercial kitchen currently under construction, which will feature seamless epoxy floors and stainless steel counters.

Next year's cleaning crews have no idea what they are in for.

•

My life in the fraternity is much, much improved. With two assistants, the food steward-related workload has been reduced to a manageable level. I make menus, compile ingredient lists, and call in food orders. Bret and Chris handle the rest.

It's heaven.

I finally have time to relax and take in the fraternity experience. My grades shoot up. My anxiety goes down.

Fraternity life for me, at last, is good.

May 1977

MIT News:

A bombshell hits the campus. Two MIT women pen a controversial article in MIT's "Thursday" newspaper. In the article, Roxanne Ritchie and Susan Gilbert rate 36 sex partners from 0 stars ("Turkey") to 4 stars ("Must fuck"). The most shocking part—the article includes the real names of all the men.

A week later, a few men are seen walking around campus with t-shirts bearing only "****".

World and Local News:

An obscure science fiction film opens nationwide on May 25th. The movie, *Star Wars*, is an immediate hit. However, its gross is dwarfed by another film opening on the same date, *Smoky and the Bandit*.

•

No members of our chapter are mentioned in the "Thursday" sex article, much to everyone's relief (or perhaps not!).[*]

---

[*] Allegedly, one member of the chapter had, in the past, experienced some "horizontal refreshment" with one of the women, and was greatly relieved to have been omitted from the article.

The media has a field day, with the story being picked up by AP, UPI, NBC, CBS, The New York Times, The Washington Post, and many others.

My (liberal) parents call and ask me "What's going on up there?"

It wasn't me!

•

At a full house meeting, we vote to change the meal preparation approach for next year. We shelve our current approach of "forced participation" to a voluntary system with monetary incentives.

FREEDOM!

I am a vocal proponent, if not the primary instigator, for this change. The new plan will increase our dues slightly, but a seat-of-the-pants estimate reveals that it should not be more than $100/year ($470), which seems like a bargain.

The new plan will pay for a breakfast cook, who will cook pancakes, French toast, bacon, and eggs on the grill to order, and a dinner cook, who will be paid about twice as much to prepare a full meal for the forty-plus brothers.

Those with the aptitude and desire to cook, and with a financial need, can sign up for a spot in the rotation. We set the pay rates to ensure an ample supply of cooks, and ensure that all who want to cook will have a chance. [*]

Al, I, and several others will take advantage of the opportunity next year. It's a part-time job for us and helps to pay for a good chunk of our fraternity dues. Food quality is vastly improved, and, in general, everyone is happy with the new arrangement.

For those who had the desire, and the ability, to cook, the job paid very reasonable wages, and could be done in their own home! Who said working from home was a modern invention?

While no "Brown v. Topeka Board of Education," our decision is one of the first where we become aware that we are setting a precedent for our chapter's future.

---

[*] Provided they are "qualified."

The reasons for our initial approach most likely stemmed from our uncertainty about what our costs would be for our first year, coupled with our "startup ethic," where everyone pulled together to make things happen.

Nonetheless, the results of our first year's "experiment" were at best, passable, and we realized we could do better by incentivizing those who were more interested and motivated to cook.

As it turns out, the house will continue to pay brothers to cook in this manner for another fifteen years, until the decision is made to hire a full-time cook.

Years later, alumni share many stories about meals cooked by brothers that failed spectacularly, and others that required superb improvisational efforts to pull off.

Meals prepared by brothers may not always have been up to the standards of a professional chef, but the quality of lasting memories is hard to beat.

•

The renovation is quickly closing in on us, threatening to swallow those of us living in the building. Fortunately, the semester ends, and people leave, preventing mass casualties.

Before leaving, some of the brothers scope out where the new wall opening will be that will connect the existing third-floor lounge to the new digs in the center section.

A plan is formulated.

Sledgehammers are fairly easy to come by on the renovation site (especially at night). After a brief midnight requisition, departing brothers assess the wall.

"Are you sure this is the right spot?"

"I told you I read the plans. The opening's right here."

"Check it again, just to make sure."

Check twice, smash once.

Location verified, brothers take turns bashing the wall.

It is both cathartic and highly enjoyable in its own sake, especially when coupled with adult beverages.

In the aftermath, they inspect the results of their hard labor.

It is good.

We envision the architects the next day, hands on their hips, looking at our finished work.

Well, I hope you're happy with yourselves!

We are.

•

It's time to say goodbye to our army surplus furniture. It's not going to go along with us to our new digs. It served us... well, it served us. At under fifty dollars total, an entire house's worth of such furniture cost less than one single new desk. It was the deal of a lifetime.

To take its place, the Institute is providing us (i.e., renting/leasing to us) brand new furniture. The furniture will also be the deal of a lifetime, but in this case, that means that it will take us a lifetime to pay it off (actually 15 years). By that time, acquiring replacement furniture will hopefully be somebody else's problem.[*]

•

Those who are staying the summer on campus (me again) are provided the opportunity to rent rooms in the completed section of the building at 355 Mass Ave.

We have to move over quickly. Workers need to start on the renovations immediately to ensure that the building is done on time.

The rear section of the first floor of the building, which will contain the two commercial kitchens, along with the deck, is not yet completed, so we can't use those kitchens in the summer.

But WILG's layout contains a smaller, upper floor, kitchen area. And that *is* ready for operation. Summer boarders will share the kitchen. We all get along swimmingly.

The newly renovated summer rooms are nice, and give us a vision for what our side will look like when it's done. Those who stay the summer will miss the "shock" of coming back in the fall and seeing the "great reveal."

---

[*] Actually, it will still be our problem, because, by that time, we will have become 'wealthy alumni' who will be asked to donate to a new furniture campaign.

Summer 1977

MIT News:

> The July summer issue of The Tech notes that the Class of '81 currently sits at 1102 people. Director of Admissions Peter Richardson states that "that number is not going to hold up," due to summer melt, and he predicts an actual size of 1080. He notes that 16% of the class are women. He adds that he is "not sure what it's going to take to change that."

World News:

> The great New York City blackout hits on July 13ᵗʰ, lasting 25 hours. Widespread looting, vandalism, and arson occur.

> The Atari 2600 is prepared for its September release in North America, for a price of $199 ($900). It is bundled with one game—*Combat*.

●

The Institute is thrilled with our first year's success. In the end-of-the-year President's report, the housing office pats themselves (somewhat forcefully) on the back, stating:

The many and difficult problems of accommodating the larger number of first-year students ever were solved with éclat by Dean Kenneth Browning and his associates. The new fraternity, Alpha Delta Phi, and the new Women's Independent Living Group had successful first years.

Hopefully, over the summer, we'll be able to figure out what this éclat thing is, and how we might be able to use it again next year.

•

With all residents finally excised, work begins on the 351 section. The renovation architects immediately come to us and ask what happened to our stairwell doors. We tell them they were "repurposed" into our dining room tables.

They are horrified.

We are informed that they were asbestos fire doors designed to keep any fires on one floor from spreading to other floors. We have violated the city fire code, in addition to increasing our fire risk.

Well maybe if you had provided us with a few friggin' folding tables, we wouldn't be in this mess.

•

At some point in the summer, the contractors approach us with an "issue." One of the female boarders living in the rear section has a habit of doing nude exercises in her room every morning.

Attention is paid. We are very intrigued.

"So, what's the problem, again?"

"The workers aren't getting any work done whiles she's... performing. It's becoming a schedule risk."

We agree to leave a note on her door, asking her to please either "put up window shades or put on clothes," at least, "until the construction is completed."

"Feel free," the note continues, "to resume your prior arrangements after that time."

•

Tom Burgmann stays the summer. At his job in Tech Square, he works the night shift from 8 pm-8 am, the only time he can access needed equipment.

The schedule requires Tom to sleep during the day.

Everyone understands.

Except for Adrian, who for some reason, needs to talk to Tom during the only time he has to sleep. Tom ignores the banging on the door.

Go away!

Adrian is undaunted. From his personal phone line, he dials the second-floor lounge. A summer resident answers.

"Is Tom Burgmann, there? It's important."

"Hold on a moment."

Tom is fetched for the important call. He walks down to the second floor and picks up the phone.

"Hello?"

"It's Adrian."

Dammit!

•

The first pledge project is undertaken. Utilizing hardwood floor pieces collected from the renovation, a bar is constructed in the former basement dining room.

A joint effort of many members of the Dirty Dozen, the bar proves eminently drink-worthy. Though it will be upgraded many times in upcoming years, the very first pledge project sets an extremely high bar for future pledge classes to meet.

Rushing Into a New Building

This was the moment we had been waiting for.

In the Wizard of Oz, there is one memorable scene where Dorothy, house transplanted by a twister, works her way through the dull, sepia interior and opens her door into a brand new world of Technicolor. It was the moment, as children, we always looked forward to.

The renovated chapter house was the Wizard of Oz scenario—in reverse. Working our way through the gray Cambridge streets and sidewalks, we reach the entrance to the building, which, at least from the front, appeared to be largely unchanged. Once entering inside, it opened into a brand-new world.

The first thing that jumped out was how clean everything was. Spotless. The carpeting was brand new. The walls were painted and unblemished. The wooden floors gleamed with a mirror finish.

The dining room, large enough to handle sixty or more brothers, had real tables and chairs. The living room had comfortable furniture.

The kitchen was simply magnificent in comparison to what we had had previously. The stainless-steel surfaces sparkled, the large refrigerators and freezers could hold enough food for weeks, the pantry was spacious. The sinks were deep enough to hold the largest pots, and the floor was, at least initially, literally clean enough to eat off of.

The dishwasher was ridiculously powerful, and the resulting dishes and glassware would be so hot that they seemed to dry themselves in seconds.

Even for those of us who had stayed the summer, the total effect of the renovated building was impressive. For those who came back to see it for the first time at the end of August, the effect was stunning.

It was simply hard to imagine that this was the same building.

•

In the Fall of '77, The Tech published a rush calendar of events. We had five rush events listed.

The first event, on Friday evening, was a repeat of last year's "beer tasting" party. In 1977, this meant something a little different than it does today.

The Tech lists our description of the event.

> ADP Beer Tasting Party - Wide selection of imported and domestic beers, including Coors, Heineken, and Michelob.

It's hard to imagine how such rare and classic beers could fail to bring droves of freshmen.

To be fair, at the time, Coors was still a relatively scarce commodity. President Ford had vaulted the beer into national prominence only a few years earlier by revealing that it was his favorite beer and that he had it flown into DC, refrigerated, so he could continue to indulge in the White House.

Heineken was the only widely available imported beer. Michelob was Anheuser-Bush's "premium" beer, marketed with the slogan "Weekends were made for Michelob!"

Still, we have to cringe today at what we thought constituted a classy "tasting" event. It also seems a little odd that MIT allowed frats to hold alcohol-themed rush events for freshmen. The drinking age was 18 at the time, but even so, viewed from our current perspective, this seemed like an invitation for trouble.

•

The rest of our lineup involved food. I think we just wanted to try out our new kitchen.

Saturday pancake brunch featured "traditional and unusual pancakes and syrups." It was obvious that our marketing whiz had been working overtime.

Our Saturday evening meal duplicated our wildly successful, New England seafood dinner from the previous year, followed by an 8 pm ice cream party, another carryover from our first successful rush.

Don't tamper with success!

Instead of the big day trip of our first year, we let our newly renovated building be the big draw. And it was. From one of the worst fraternity physical structures, we now had, almost certainly, the finest accommodations on campus. Our tours were grand and glorious.

Our only Sunday event was a cookout on the new patio. Since the patio was a shared space with WILG, we had to negotiate events that used the facility. We only had one hard and fast rule.

Keep your cat off the patio!

•

What to talk about with candidates, besides "Where are you from," was always a challenge for many of us who weren't naturally gifted conversationalists.

I recall talking with one freshman, Jon Moon, and coming away with an interesting take. Jon asked me my shoe size.

That's a new one.

Jon wore size 13 shoes, so when he was invariably asked, in return, for his shoe size, it started an interesting conversation.

During our chat, he talked about his family business, which I believe was farming, and how they had taken out various loans.

I asked him why they took out loans (or maybe a line of credit) when they didn't need them.

He explained that you always want to get a loan before you

need it, because if you wait until you need one, you'll no longer qualify, and then you're screwed. I thought that was a very fine observation, and it has stuck with me to this day.

Give that man a bid!

•

Our first rush in the renovated building was an unqualified success. Our beer and food-themed events, combined with the impressive new building interior, seemed to hit the "sweet spot" with incoming students, as we pledged a total of 25, almost certainly the highest total of any of the 31 fraternities. The "ADPLO" pledge class, after more than forty years, still appears to be our chapter's largest pledge class.

Somewhere around 360 freshmen and transfer students pledge one of MIT's 31 fraternities, with our share about seven percent of that total, or more than double that of the average frat.

That's an impressive rush.

A Brief Look Into the Future

The next year, Andy and Tom Burgmann unleash a new slew of pledge training and pre-initiation rituals.

Tom, true to his early impression during rush week, was finally able to take a large role in "creating traditions."

Maybe we should have dialed him back a bit.

•

In October, we finally get our first Constitution. Apparently, we'd been living in the lawless old west our entire first year. The position of Sheriff is finally abolished.

Kevin Ossler is president and the prime mover behind the effort. He creates a very thorough and detailed document, complete with by-laws, amendments, and a bill of rights. The new Constitution is rammed through ~~Congress~~ the house in record time.

It even has a clause prohibiting "ex post facto" rules and regulations. All first-year would-be criminals breathe a sigh of relief.

●

A few years later, a new pledge manual will appear. It's nearly one hundred pages total. Kevin Ossler also appears to be the architect of this epic tome. It's evident that from his body of work that he had a love for governing and documenting our fraternal journey. It's a wonderfully informative effort, but I pity the new pledges that must learn all of this.

I wonder if they sell Cliff's Notes.

●

In Spring of '78, ADP competes in the inaugural "Tank-Team" speed beer-drinking competition on the Kresge Oval, as part of MIT's Kaleidoscope Celebration. Todd Hubing, who never drank before coming to MIT, is astounded that he's progressed so far that he's now part of our ten-member drinking team. And even more astounded that MIT would sanction such an event, even for a charitable cause.

The goal is for each team member to down his pint, followed immediately by the next member, and so on down the line, all within 35 seconds for the ten pints. Carl Heinzl anchors the team and is said to be able to down a pint faster than gravity allows. Fortunately, for our team, Carl has still not yet passed freshman physics, which allows him to accomplish such a feat.

A few years later, Massachusetts passes a state law prohibiting alcoholic consumption under contest conditions. For some reason, participation in future Tank competitions begins to tank.

●

Jon Cohen recalls that while he was dating one of the WILG members, he grew tired of having to go all the way from his fourth-floor room down to the front entrance, then across to the 355 entrance, and back up the stairs to the fourth floor of WILG.

A much more direct way was simply to go through the center stairway landing. But the doors were fire exits, and an alarm would go off when the door was opened.

Fed up with his long jaunts, Jon surreptitiously taped over the battery contacts on the alarms for the two fourth-floor doors. His plan worked perfectly for quite some time.

Some of the WILG members began to ask him, "How'd you get over here so fast?"

Jon just smiled.

Eventually, Bob Glatz, house manager, tests the fire doors and tries to figure why the fourth-floor door alarms are malfunctioning. The presence of tape over the battery contacts sets off an internal alarm bell. He hypothesizes that the fault may have been due to human intervention.

Jon's shortcut is short-circuited.

Busted!

•

At some point during the next year, the chapter still possessed the traveling trophy. As required, it is displayed in a prominent location, which in our new facility was the second-floor living room.

Tom Burgmann, in much the same fashion as Jon the year before, rigs up a trophy alarm system, now fashioned from spare fire alarms.

Inevitably, an attempt is made on the trophy. This time, as the alarm goes off, the thieves drop it off the living room balcony to waiting-accomplices outside, and they make off with it.

At the time, Tom is the undergraduate governor of Alpha Delta Phi, a great honor for himself and our chapter. As governor, one of his duties involves attending the International conventions. And the next convention, in Madison, Wisconsin, is right around the corner. Bob Glatz is the other student representative from our chapter. Todd Hubing, who hails from Madison, makes the trip also.

Tom's reasonably confident that the trophy is going to make an appearance at the convention. As he arrives at the hotel, he looks up and sees a familiar sight.

High up in an upper-floor hotel room, on the window ledge, visible to everyone entering the convention, sits *our* trophy. They're boasting to all the other chapters that they've got it in their possession.

This will not be tolerated.

The trio hatch a plan, so deviously simple that most people

possessing their intellectual capacity would have simply overlooked it.

They figure that the hotel is swamped with undergrads from everywhere, often drunk, who frequently misplace their keys. The overworked hotel clerks don't have time to check out each story.

After determining the room number that contained the statue, Tom boldly strides up to the front desk.

"I lost my key for room ___," could I get another?"

"Sure," came the reply, along with a brand-new key.

Waiting until they are reasonably certain the room is unoccupied, our group strolls into the room and re-appropriates the trophy. Of course, they make sure to carry it into the convention hall for all to see.

Score one more for Lambda Phi.

•

Despite the ban on large water-fighting equipment, a huge battle breaks out in the first year of the newly renovated building. The members of the battle club have dubbed themselves the "Junior Firefighters' League."

Realizing they are about to get sanctioned for violating the new rules against large-scale water-arms, they decide their best hope is to confess en masse, promising to disband their League and to "never let this happen again."

Their ploy is successful, setting a dangerous precedent for dealing with future acts of mass civil disobedience.

•

Relations with WILG seem to run the gamut from fantastic to "I'm not speaking to those people, right now."

During good times, the rear kitchen and patio doors are open, or at least unlocked, allowing free access to either side. A locked door—usually by WILG—usually indicated that the other side has committed a perceived offense.

On one occasion, Jeff Thiemann and another brother enter the WILG kitchen and remove all the labels from their cans. Instead of simply leaving WILG cooks to stare at blank metal cans, they thoughtfully place a letter code on the cans—e.g., "A" for tomato sauce cans, "B" for green beans, etc.—so that the cans' contents can be deciphered—only, however, after one can of each type was opened.

It was never officially verified that WILG's next meal consisted of spaghetti and meatballs in a delicious fruit cocktail sauce.

Bafflingly, after this incident, WILG locked its doors for quite some time.

Jeff simply wanted to encourage a "can-do" attitude.

•

Despite any tensions with WILG, there were always social interactions on a personal basis between fraternity brothers and WILG members.

Pam Thiemann recalls, that at one time, she and two other fourth-floor WILG members, Michelle and Nancy, were all dating ADP third-floor brothers.

All three couples eventually married, making Jeff and Pam Thiemann, Bob and Michelle Glatz, and Todd and Nancy Hubing among the first members of each group to expand the ADP-WILG connection well outside institutional boundaries.

•

Rob Mandel takes a year off from MIT. At one point, he sends a telegram to the frat, which is read at a house meeting.

Rob is aware that many telegrams used the word "STOP" instead of a period at the end of a sentence.

The content of Rob's telegram ended with this:

"...Wishing you the best. Bye. Hope you will stop by."

As transmitted, in all caps, the telegram became:

"...WISHING YOU THE BEST STOP BYE STOP HOPE YOU WILL STOP BY STOP"

Rob's message achieved its desired goal of thoroughly confusing everyone in attendance.

There's no stopping Rob, even when he's hundreds of miles away.

Stop.

•

At some point, Brothers Dave Jilk and Mark Stiffler, hanging around the second-floor landing, "rediscover" the fact that, underneath many layers of paint, there is attractive hardwood. This ultimately leads to a project to strip the paint for the entire stairwell, taking the stairwell's appearance to a completely new level.

•

Rob Mandel's "Alpha Delt Fund for Laundering, Cleaning, and Immaculatory Operations" is later renamed "Lambda Phi Vending Services" (LPVS) as it also includes more washers and dryers, a soda (pop) machine, and possibly other coin-operated vending machines.

The LPVS is very profitable and builds a sizable surplus. At one point, a $5,000 loan is made to the Michigan ADP chapter from LPVS funds, in an apparent snub by Kevin Ossler to the International.

•

For the next few years, the kitchen is kept in pristine condition by scrupulous after-dinner clean-up inspections. Bret and Chris establish the precedent, verifying that every surface is clean.

But their successor, Ron Tyler, takes the job to another level. Every surface and every nook and cranny *must* be spotless.

No exceptions!

The nightly show is very entertaining for those not involved directly in the night's cleanup. Some come down just to watch.

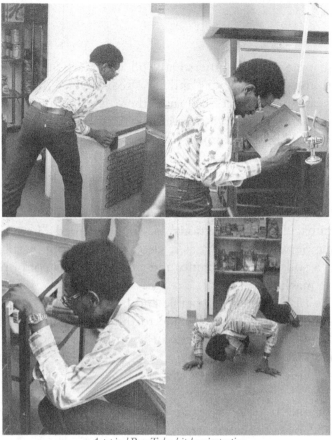

A typical Ron Tyler kitchen inspection

Memories

I actually miss the smell of Necco wafers in the morning. It smells like ADP – Brad Feld

•

Soon after Mike "Corky" Corcoran helped us get started in his role as Alpha Delt field representative, he moved on to a successful career in the telecom industry. He also quit drinking immediately after his field rep days and hasn't touched a drop since, although he does admit he had a "wonderful" time before he quit.

Mike, who dropped the "Corky" moniker along with the distilled spirits, recalls that despite his initial skepticism, he came to the opinion that MIT had the best students of any of the colleges he worked with, and that second place "wasn't even close."

Why thank you very much.

He noted that MIT students had a deep-seated curiosity and desire to learn, even outside of the STEM fields.

He also recounted one of his favorite fraternity stories. A few years back, his adult daughter and some friends were going to be in the Boston area. Before leaving, he suggested that she drop by and visit our chapter, since he was involved in its start.

His daughter found the building and knocked on the door. She told the brothers who answered who she was, and that her father was Mike Corcoran.

"Mike Corcoran. *The Mike Corcoran*! Oh my God! Come on in!"

His daughter recalls that she and her group were treated like royalty.

She left with a newfound respect for her dad.

•

Russ Kalis recounted a strikingly similar story to that of Mike. His daughter stopped by, unannounced. She was greeted at the door, and when she presented her "credentials," the brothers present were thrilled. Word spread quickly.

"Russ Kalis' daughter is here!"

She was quickly ushered in, and also given the royal treatment. This, too, made a big impression on his daughter.

Your old man was not too shabby, back in the day.

Russ wasn't one for the big city. As soon as each semester was over, he headed back home to Minnesota. But the fraternity was a refuge.

He recalls that the living conditions of the first year, and the need to work together in our startup environment, helped develop a sense of comradery. Regular trips to Fathers – just down the street seemed to strengthen the bond.

The first year, we were "figuring out who we were."

He fondly remembers the Necco plant across the street. With one whiff, you could tell which type of wafer was being cooked that day.

Wintergreen was always my favorite.

•

Steve Ofsthun is remembered as one of the friendliest and kindest members of the first pledge class. He was also one of our best athletes, running hurdles on the track team, and he was the go-to person to get our IM teams prepped for battle.

On at least one Thanksgiving, he invited brothers up to his family home in Buffalo to celebrate the holiday.

Steve had had experience working in a pizza parlor back home and instigated a house pizza party where he instructed brothers on the proper technique for tossing the dough.

It's all in the wrists.

He also instructed us about the proper preparation of what was becoming a national fad at the time, "buffalo wings."

A very unpretentious and giving person, Steve volunteered to get Rob Mandel in shape for Army boot camp during the summer.

And he did.

•

Bob Anderson never seemed to get angry. Bob was gay, but not fully "out" during his time at the frat. It was the norm for the times. Most of the brothers, including myself, didn't seem to realize.

Jon Cohen recalls, reflecting the culture of the times, that we occasionally made what would be considered today to be homophobic jokes. If this bothered Bob, he didn't let on. He was always friendly, helpful, cheerful, and, most of all, kind.

Bob loved champagne. He hosted tasting parties in the lounge. Champagne was part of our social events. On several occasions, he assembled a group to head over to the Hyatt Regency to sample some champagne. One glass per person was all we could afford back then.

Bob volunteered his time even after graduating, coming to help in workweek projects. It was in his nature to help.

I recall Bob asking me to review one of his econ papers, or maybe it was his thesis. It was about the issues related to electronic funds transfers, a promising new technology that had yet to go mainstream way back in 1977.

Bob was ahead of his time.

Bob Anderson dancing on the sidewalk in front of the chapter house and doing his best pantsless Tom Cruise impersonation during a Risky Business party.

•

Rob Mandel recalls that he initially wanted to join the frat because he was looking for a consistent social group, in contrast with dorms, in which life at times could be alienating, and friends would come and go.

People in the dorms where he lived, when approached for help, would sometimes tell you what you needed to know, but it was often done condescendingly—as in: "that should be intuitively obvious."

It was quite a different experience with his fraternity brothers. While there was always friendly kidding, when help was requested, it was provided without the need to make you feel inferior.

It seemed like a minor thing, but it turns out that it was vitally important. Being part of a group with shared values and being thought of as someone worthy of consideration made all the difference.

Rob's a realist—he remembers that the frat could be noisy and crowded. It was very hot in the summer, and the food was often mediocre.*

But he loved it.

A dense population of personable geniuses had many advantages. Rob could get up a group any time and just go out someplace. Or he could just hang out and shoot the breeze with brothers who were brilliant, interesting, witty, and opinionated.

Just like himself!

Rob Mandel cooking up some grub in the new kitchen.

•

Bob Glatz fondly recalled his time living in the frat. In

---

* Rob's memory is suspect in this area.

addition to beer, athletics, and social events, he recalls that, somewhat amazingly, a vast amount of learning also went on.

In the event of a question or problem with his Course 2 curriculum, he could wander over to another mechanical engineer's room and get some priceless help. In turn, especially as an upperclassman, he was able to return the favor.

Bob remembered that Bob Anderson served as a "phenomenal" mentor to both Todd Hubing and himself. Need help picking out a suit for an interview—Bob Anderson would be there to assist. Most importantly, Bob Anderson helped many brothers to transition into a more accepting attitude toward gay people.

Bob Glatz also recounted that we used to buy one bottle of expensive alcohol, then refill it with the cheap stuff. When I told him that I still use that technique, his opinion of me went down several notches.

You're not supposed to do that when you're no longer a cheap-ass broke college student.

Six months after he graduated, Bob visited the frat, and for old-times sake, went back to Father's for a beer. He now found the $1 pitchers that he used to consume in vast quantities to be "undrinkable swill."

Little did he know that this was a test.

He had passed.

Bob had successfully made the transition into the "real world."

•

I only lived at the chapter house for two years. I left the frat after my junior year to get married.

I can still recall the house meeting when I announced that I would be getting married, and the warm reception and encouragement I got from all the brothers at the time. Many snaps. That was a nice feeling.

A few weeks later, a surprise bachelor party was held in the living room. It was quite the affair, complete with entertainment commensurate with the times and... various other interesting occurrences. While not my preferred celebratory choice at the time, the sentiment behind it was greatly appreciated.

After my first semester, which was just too much work, life at the chapter house was, for me, a grand experience.

One brother recalls that I was quiet and kept to myself, and I'm sure I was, but from my perspective, it didn't feel that way.

Something interesting was always going on in the chapter house. And someone interesting was always available to talk to. I was soaking it in. And I always felt a part of it.

So much so, that even over forty years later, I have recurring dreams (nightmares?) about going back to Cambridge and/or MIT and living at the frat. In my dreams, I'm constantly searching for my room, walking down seemingly infinite hallways to find wherever it is I'm supposed to be sleeping.

Apparently, I'm not alone. In the email discussion group, Andy Bronstein related similar nocturnal housing forays. His suggestion: the current house manager should set aside a room designated for alumni brothers to occupy in their dreams.

Amen, brother, amen.

The author sweats out his bachelor party, much to the amusement of Tom Burgmann, as Jim Leary looks on.

Dealing With Demographics

In 1976, the original ten members could not envision where the fraternity would be in a decade's time, not to mention in two, three, or four decades, or, at the time of this writing, some forty-five years later.

Two of the original ten are deceased. Bob Anderson passed away in 2004, and Steve Ofsthun in 2018.

Most of us understood that our renovated chapter house would someday hold over fifty members, a total surpassed only two years later, after hugely successive rushes totaling 25 and 17 pledges, respectively.

I don't believe any of us envisioned the house hitting 62 (63?) members as it did in 1998, a situation that saw the chapter house so full that two brothers had to make do by using the basement pub as a double—subsequently named the "Den of Sin."

We could not have foreseen what happened to fraternities in 2002, when, as a result of the hazing death of a Phi Gamma pledge in 1997, the Institute decided that all freshmen would be required to spend their first year in the dormitory.

This ruling appeared to immediately set our chapter size on a downward trajectory, from 50-60 brothers down to below 20 only five years later, as detailed in the chart that follows. To help increase revenue during this time, the chapter began renting to non-member boarders.[*]

Alumni involvement after Decade Three in 2006 helped to reverse the trend and the fraternity recovered impressively over the next decade.

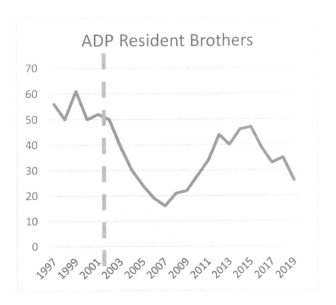

But another emerging demographic shift threatened to create even more pressure on fraternity's numbers.

●

None of us in our first year, including Dean of Admissions Peter Richardson, foresaw the Institute's commitment to gender parity in undergraduate admissions. The female percentage of undergraduates rose from 16% in 1976 to a figure of nearly 50% today.

These two factors – freshman living on campus, and the declining male undergraduate population—combined for a one-two punch that threatened the viability of many fraternities. Our

---

[*] "Boarders" are actually renters who have kitchen privileges but buy and prepare their own food.

chapter was not exempt.

In 1976, there were around 3,500 male undergraduates who were fraternity eligible. In 2020, the number was around 1,700—almost exactly half.

The thirty-or-so MIT fraternities must compete with a shrinking base. Some of the fraternities became coed, instantly doubling the population from which they could draw upon.

But many others, including ADP, remained all-male. A "macro" view of current undergraduate demographics leads to the inescapable conclusion—most, if not all, the exclusively male fraternities—are going to be far under capacity.

●

One additional factor combines to make filling the house even more difficult. As all MIT freshmen spend the first year in the dorm, they make social connections that, in many cases, make them less receptive to fraternity life.

Brother Steve Bergstein points out that we now regularly deal with depledging, and brothers who pledge and are initiated, but who decide not to move into the house.

> ...we previously had little experience of pledges depledging and very, very little experience of newly initiated brothers not living in the house, both things happen with much more frequency since the pledges generally live in dorms where they establish social networks.
>
> When they're not living in the house, it can be easy to back-burner the fraternity as school and dorm friends consume time and mindshare.
>
> With an established social circle in a dorm, there's good reason to stay there, with dorm friends, [for the] sophomore year. It's a challenge to compete against that. We've been telling pledges that we expect them to move in as sophomores, but there's no real way for us to enforce this post-initiation.

Competition for the now greatly reduced male undergraduate base is extreme. This, along with societal shifts, means that fraternities are forced to compete—at least in part—based on the services they provide.

MIT tuition in 1976 was $4,000, or around $19,000 in today's dollars. MIT tuition in 2021 is nearly $54,000. For their money, today's students may expect to receive more, and this extends to their living situation as well.

And in today's society in general, the average individual expects more services than was the case in 1976. Appealing to undergrads through the promise of shared work experiences and bonding is an admirable goal, but such a recruitment strategy will most likely struggle to be competitive against other frats touting a more pleasurable fraternity experience.

The building and location are only a part of a fraternity's attraction. Fraternities also compete on the quality of food they provide. Although some living groups, such as WILG, still pay resident volunteers to cook, for most fraternities, if not all, full-time paid chefs are a distinct selling point.

•

As opposed to the mostly "locally-owned-and-operated" chapter of the '70s era, today, the "The Friends of the Lambda Phi Chapter of the Alpha Delta Phi Fraternity" Corporation, staffed by alumni, oversees much of the chapter's operations.

Budgets, rapidly approaching $500K/year, are submitted and vetted by the board. Dues are paid through OmegaFi, an online financial system, which also provides a variety of financial services to the chapter and Board.

The Board's closer oversight provides several advantages. As past board president Steve Bergstein reflects, it provides a way to keep alumni involved:

> We have a bunch of alumni now, many of whom like the opportunity to continue to be connected in a regular way to the house.

It also reflects the changing cultural environment. Bergstein comments about the changes he's seen from his days as a freshman in 1983 when there was a great deal more "do-it-yourself" emphasis.

A lot has changed, too. No freshmen in the house. Much less skill and much less interest in DIY (this is the case system-wide) than in my day.

MIT now requires a graduate resident advisor "GRA" to live in each fraternity. The Institute keeps a much closer tab on all fraternities than was the case in earlier times.

•

Although it's tempting to look back to the "good old days," and wonder why today's undergraduates aren't willing to put in the effort we did, we have to realize that we can't fight the current culture.

Fraternity values and experiences can be preserved even in the new era, and there are a lot of advantages as a current undergraduate in our house.

Our current website details a list of chapter features, including all single rooms, dinners prepared by Chef John for five nights a week, pub, hot tub, workroom, game room, tv room, library/piano room, and more.

Sounds like a place I might be interested in.

Reconnecting

I only lived at the chapter house for two years. As mentioned earlier, I left the frat after my junior year to get married.

All the brothers were invited, and those who were around that summer came to my wedding in Bedford, MA.

As you can tell from the photo, at the time, things were definitely "looking up."

Our new residence was a bit up the street—a one-bedroom apartment at 863 Mass Ave. I had to walk by the chapter house on my way to campus every day, so very often I'd meet people from the house on the way and we'd walk down together.

I also had to walk through Central Square, past the McDonalds located there. On one occasion, Brother Ed McNack happened to be eating there, looking out the window. He spotted me walking by. According to Ed, I had a huge grin on my face.

The next time I saw him, he told me my grin made me look like one of the mentally disturbed people who frequented the city streets on occasion.

I told him that I often came up with puns and wordplay as I walked, and since this was the first time I had heard them myself, I reacted appropriately.

"Uh-huh."

Ed's side-eye glance led me to believe he wasn't entirely convinced.

•

Kevin Ossler, who pledged my last year in the house, and George Gruetzmacher, from the following pledge class, did their best to keep me in the loop over the next few years.

We'd occasionally have frat members over to our small apartment "just up the street."

But it's harder for people such as myself, not naturally outgoing, to keep in touch on a continuing basis.

•

The next year, we moved to Watertown, I began work at Hewlett Packard Medical Products, then in Waltham. I imagine some overtures were made regarding chapter initiations and banquets, but I have no recollection of them.

A few years later, in 1982, my eldest son was born, and a year after that we moved down to Florida. As mentioned, it was harder to keep track of people back then, and I just "lost touch."

Apparently, there was a Decade One reunion in 1986, but I have no memory that I was even aware of it, and only a vague recollection of being cognizant of Decade Two.

Decade Three happened in 2006. George Gruetzmacher called me just a few weeks before the event to personally invite me. Based on his call, I decided to go.

The list of speakers at Decade Three was a little ad hoc. Adrian Zuckerman got up and talked for a while and then motioned for me to come up to the podium to say a few words. I looked around, hoping to see someone seated right behind me.

Please don't let it be me.

It was me.

Public speaking and I go together kind of like toothpaste and orange juice. It can be done, but it's not pleasant, and it tends to leave a lingering bad aftertaste.

So, I just started talking. Thankfully, I've blanked most of it out. But I do remember, at one point, I was recounting some story about our startup, and I was thinking out loud about how long ago it all was.

"I think it's been..., yeah, it's been thirty years!"

Much chuckling from the audience. I looked around.

What's everyone laughing at?

Then it dawned on me. The giant banner on the wall. Every single announcement for this event. Decade Three—the thirtieth anniversary of the start of our chapter—was the whole reason behind the reunion.

I suppose the one positive thing about this was that I had independently derived the solution and come up with the correct answer.

This made an impression on my younger Lambda Phi progeny in the audience. It was clear I had become one of those "old codgers" who wasn't quite all there.

After the speakers were finished, some of the current members of the "Pelham Family" came up to me.

"Hello, Mr. Pelham," they said, speaking slowly and deliberately, carefully pronouncing every syllable. "Could...we...get...a...picture...with...you?"

They showed me a phone and made large, exaggerated, pantomimed motions of pushing the shutter. They even made shutter-clicking noises.

"See? It will take our picture."

I was humbled, and not in a good way.

•

Tony Pelham, Al Mink, Louis Cohen, Adrian Zuckerman, Bob Wolf, and Steve Ofsthun from the "Original Ten" pledge class, at Decade III.

Louis, Al, and Tony reenact the original ADP party. Where are the munchies?

•

Decade Four came, shockingly, only a few years after Decade Three. Or so it seems, as the perception of elapsed time appears to correlate inversely to age.

The brothers I knew from my years at the house all looked

noticeably older now.

"What's happened to them?" I said to myself.

After the event, I looked at the pictures of the pledge classes taken at the reunion.

"Who's that old balding guy?"

Then, of course, came the realization.

It was me.

At Decade Four, for the first time that I can recall, the older alumni seemed very aware of their mortality. We were all approaching the big six-0. A few were already past it. It began to dawn on us that by Decade Five, it was likely that a few of us would no longer be around.

It wasn't quite yet to the point of "look to your left, look to your right—one of you won't be here," but statistically, we could expect around a ten percent death rate over the next decade for the oldest pledge classes.

Of course, in general, we take care of ourselves better than the average person. But out of the sixty remaining brothers of the first four pledge classes, the statistics tell us the expected number of mortalities could reach as high as six.

As of this writing, nearly halfway through the decade, we've had one death—Steve Ofsthun.

Tony Pelham, Steve Ofsthun Al Mink, Adrian Zuckerman, Bob Wolf, Jon Cohen, and Rob Mandel from the "Original Ten" pledge class, at Decade IV.

•

I struggled with how much of my personal "story" to include in this chapter and ultimately decided to leave almost all of it out. It will suffice to say that at times in the past, I've counted myself as one of our alumni "failures." Or at least, not a "success story."

I no longer think that, but my life's trajectory has given me an appreciation for the fact that a great deal of our experience is often a result of circumstances, timing, and other events (or genetics) beyond our control.

I am fortunate to be resilient enough to weather some of the more difficult times, but not everyone is so fortunate.

And I wish I had been able to keep in better touch with my fraternity brothers over the years, but, for whatever reasons, it didn't happen that way.

Fortunately, life moves forward, and as far as reconnecting with fraternity brothers, technology has come to the rescue.

Electronic Bonds

At the time of the fraternity's founding, most of us had seen a glimpse of the future. It didn't come from the best futurists of the time or even the top science fiction writers, it came by way of a comic strip—in the form of Dick Tracy's two-way wrist radio, later upgraded to include TV.

Chester Gould, the writer of Dick Tracy, had predicted personal, electronic communication, along with continual connectedness, way back in 1945.

It just took a little while to get here.

•

At the time of our chapter's conception, if you wanted to get in touch with someone, you had three major options:

Visit them in person, call them up on the phone, or mail them a letter.

Electronic mail, as a concept, did exist, and an early version was implemented at MIT, in our own backyard, in 1965, where users who were logged into the same time-shared computer could send messages to each other.

But it wasn't until the mid-70s that the first email standards were approved, and it wasn't until the end of the '80s that email would become widely available.

•

So, for at least the first decade after our first pledge classes graduated, keeping in touch generally meant a phone call or a letter, and frequent personal visits could only be made to those who lived in the same general area.

And unless one lived in the Boston area, even the most gregarious, social, and outgoing brothers didn't see other brothers in person very often.

Right now, as I write this, we are still in the throes of the COVID-19 pandemic, so most of us don't see *anybody* in-person very often.

Most 'brotherly' communication occurs today in electronic form.

Brother Tim Gorton set up most/all of our chapter's website and wiki organization. He also created a variety of email groups through which alumni could keep in touch.

By far the most trafficked seems to be the Lambda Phi "discussion" email group.

The group collectively represents the combined knowledge and experience of all Lambda Phi alumni. It's an impressive body of knowledge and a frequent source of wisdom and advice.

Brother Dave Jilk serves as something of an unofficial discussion orchestrator.

Almost any question posed to the group is returned with answers from one, or more likely, many brothers with experience, expertise, and or specific domain knowledge concerning the topic at hand.

It's also a news source concerning our chapter, and about specific alumni. Some news, such as the reporting of an alumni death, is shocking, and a flood of tributes and memories pour forth from brothers who had been a part of that person's life.

The discussion group provides a way to share memories, and collective grief, after such a death.

•

Requests for historical information from the discussion group can trigger a flood of memories. For purposes of this book, I wanted to find out when the chapter first hired a paid cook [answer: '89 or '90]. I sent out a request to the group.

Not only did I received the answer to my question, but the thread contained a huge number of stories relating to 'meals gone wrong' that happened when various brothers prepared the meals. Most common were those related to frozen turkeys. It appears as if some sort of turkey-related meal catastrophe was experienced at least once by every pledge class.

Although the consensus was that meal quality improved after we hired our first 'real' chef, Bobby Mac, Brother Lawrence Waugh posited that the "occasional horrific meal was part of the fraternity experience."

At least in terms of memories, many meal flops do last a lifetime.

•

On political topics, the results are much more of a mixed bag.

My take on it is that every Lambda Phi alum, after leaving the friendly confines of MIT, is used to being "the smartest guy in the room."

When we encounter a brother with a political opinion that runs 180-degrees counter to ours, our first inclination, after our initial incredulity, of course, from *someone who should know better*, is to batter them senseless with logical arguments as to why their position just might be, I don't know, utterly and unmistakably wrong, and pig-headedly and irredeemably stupid.

The problem is that every one of us thinks our arguments are logical, fact-based, and common-sensical and that the simple remedy for someone who doesn't agree with us is to explain how their arguments are not any of the above.

The threads tend to devolve into a back-and-forth flame-fest where no one changes their opinion, and feelings can get heated.

Brother Mark Scheutz gave a wonderful bit of advice to all who get involved in any type of discussion, from author Ray Dalio:

> Instead of trying to "prove" your points in the debate, spend a lot more time and energy trying to disprove what you currently believe to be true. If you can find disconfirming evidence of your current beliefs then your understanding of the truth of the matter will improve greatly and rapidly.

This seems to me to be great advice in general and useful in just about every situation where a difference of opinions pops up.

As a fan of logical discourse, I've, in the past, been accused of being "extremely blunt." In one podcast I recently heard, someone accused their spousal partner of being a 'logic bully.'

I am guilty.

While I don't think logical arguments are wrong, sometimes brute-force logic is not what people need or want to hear. And sometimes, more often than we may want to admit, our "logical" arguments are based on biases that we are not aware of.

Brother Carl Heinzl's email signature sums it up best for me.

> 'Be kinder than necessary, for everyone you meet is fighting some kind of battle'

I've been on both ends of that statement, so, nowadays, I try to remember to practice a moment of self-reflection before hitting 'Send.'

Measures of Success

To celebrate MIT's 150th anniversary in 2011, the Boston Globe publishes a special section highlighting the "150 fascinating, fun, important, interesting, lifesaving, life-altering, bizarre and bold ways that MIT has made a difference."

Among the many, many, highlights over the century-and-a-half history of the Institute, only a single fraternity was listed.

Number 140: Not "Animal House" *

Only at MIT does a single fraternity, Alpha Delta Phi, produce venture capitalists (Brad Feld, a founder of the TechStars program for aspiring entrepreneurs), videogame innovators ("Rock Band" developer Eran Egozy), public company CEOs (Colin Angle of iRobot), flying car inventors (Carl Dietrich of Terrafugia), and solar power innovators (Frank van Mierlo, CEO of 1366 Technologies). Oracle recently paid $1 billion for ATG, a Cambridge e-commerce software company founded by, yes, two former brothers

---

* There was a much closer connection to Animal House than the author realized.

216

of the ADP fraternity house, Jeet Singh and Joe Chung.[22]

Of course, an article from 2011 is necessarily out-of-date. Astronaut Dan Tani, and Ambassador to Romania Adrian Zuckerman, at least, would have been added to any current list.

And Loren Kohnfelder could have easily made the list. His bachelor's thesis in 1978 introduced numerous concepts that are now important parts of the public key cryptography infrastructure. [23]

That one of MITs newer fraternities could achieve so many huge success stories in, at that time, only 35 years of existence seems hugely improbable.

Of course, like "Man bites dog," we wouldn't be reading about it in the Boston Globe if it weren't highly unusual, and hence, newsworthy.

•

It's always dangerous to highlight only a few individuals as representative of success. For every success mentioned in the Globe article, there are dozens more Lambda Phi success stories—leaders in government, business, and the military, entrepreneurs, philanthropists, human-rights activists, educators, scientists, physicians, attorneys, engineers, authors, and even members of the MIT poker team that was widely publicized in a book and a movie.

One of the biggest successes is the ongoing work of the alumni who serve on the "Friends of the Lambda Phi" Board. Changing demographics at MIT has meant the board has had to take a larger role in the operations of the chapter house than in the earlier years.

Members of the board work behind the scenes to oversee chapter finances, plan infrastructure improvements, interface with the MIT administration, coordinate fundraising efforts, and organize reunions, among many other tasks.

And they coordinated the involved effort required to finally

---

[22]
http://archive.boston.com/news/education/higher/specials/mit150/mitlist/?page=22
[23] https://en.wikipedia.org/wiki/Loren_Kohnfelder

purchase the building from MIT.

The work of the board members in preserving and facilitating the ongoing operation of the chapter is another huge success story.

•

If the three of us, in April of 1976, or the ten of us, in September of that year, or even the twenty-two of us, a year later, had been tasked to "create the most successful MIT fraternity," it's not clear what decisions we would have made—or could have made—differently.

What is clear is that our initial pledge classes formed the core of a group that enabled us to build a chapter with tremendous diversity, along many dimensions—straight and gay, black, white, and Asian, Jewish, Christian and atheist, Republican, Democrat, and libertarian, and many other metrics.

Many brothers have mentioned this "melting pot" as one of the best things about our chapter.

•

There are quite literally thousands of motivational quotes referring to 'success.' I've read quite a few in the process of writing this chapter.

Only one made the cut.

Formula for success: rise early, work hard, strike oil.

J. Paul Getty

In our earliest efforts to build the chapter, we worked hard to find the best people we could. We were extremely fortunate.

We struck oil.

•

There is a long-running debate regarding whether or not we possess what's commonly referred to as "free will." The term "libertarian" in this context refers to those who believe that we possess such a thing, as contrasted with those who believe the opposite— "determinists."

I am a "hard" determinist. My understanding is that all our

actions, thoughts, and decisions, are determined by our brain's neural 'wiring,' and that in turn was determined by our genetics and the sum of our experiences in life—family, friends, schools, locations, situations, etc.

In fact, I am currently involved in the writing of a yet-to-be-released book dealing with this subject.*

But one doesn't have to be a hard determinist to admit that we have little to no control over many factors of our lives.

None of us can say that we had any part in choosing our intelligence, or our personalities, or our temperaments.

Likewise, none of us chose our families, where we were born, where we went to school (at least in the earliest years), what kinds of kids went to that school, who were the neighborhood kids who lived around us, and on and on.

The situations that drive our decisions, whether these are of our own volition or not, come about almost entirely from factors outside our control.

Likewise, our fraternity chapter exists, in its current form, and in every intermediate form that it has taken, in a large part, due to these external factors.

A review of the Lambda Phi chapter's history highlights some of the most important influences and drivers of our chapter's creation.

- MIT needed revenues, which necessitated increasing the undergraduate enrollment, which exacerbated their undergraduate housing situation.
- They had access to an apartment building in their Northgate portfolio which could be repurposed to address some of their housing issues.
- Coincident with this, the ADP International organization had a desire to expand.
- Henry Leeb's history and past efforts provided a "bridge" between the two factors.
- The HUD loan program most likely made the building feasible to use as student housing in a period

---

* " The Determined Life - A 'How-To' Guide to Having No Free Will"

of extraordinary interest rates.

- In 1907, Rufus William Lamson decided to build The Lamson building in the ongoing expansion of the Cambridgeport area following the bridging of the Charles River.

The list could continue as far as we wish to take it.

Without any one of these factors in place, the Lambda Phi Chapter, at least the one we know, does not exist.

•

At one point, in the Spring of 1976, the success of our chapter seemed to hinge on the efforts of three undergraduates.

At the time, however, we were only partially aware of the many other concerned entities that were hovering around us.

- The Institute was there—they wanted and needed us to succeed, providing us with a building ready for occupancy.* They provided a financial path for our members to afford to live there and eventually own the building.
- The International fraternity was there—they provided startup funds, organizational assistance, and sent their field rep to provide help to our earliest startup efforts.
- Alumni from other chapters were there—assisting with recruiting, rush, and training.
- The remaining seven members of the first pledge class were already there—living on campus at the time, soon to be joined in our effort.
- The second pledge class was there—already starting their plans for their first year at MIT.

All we had to do was to tap into these reservoirs and stand back as their contents rushed out.

•

---

* Furniture not included.

And it worked—we saw success after success. Our first ten members—the building occupied—our first rush that doubled our size—building renovations completed—our next rush where we doubled in size again.

Our chapter was thriving.

The oil was gushing.

Perhaps our earliest roles in the house's formation were particularly pivotal, but we were no more instrumental to our chapter's success than any other brother who has lived in the house and, by their presence and participation, contributed to its ongoing success.

I was fortuitously present at the time when the fraternity got off the ground, and where my contributions could be utilized as a part of the process of creating something that would ultimately prove to be of great benefit to so many of us.

•

The 'Ship of Theseus' is a well-known thought experiment. What happens when every part of a ship has eventually been replaced? Is it still the same ship?

> The ship wherein Theseus and the youth of Athens returned from Crete had thirty oars, and was preserved by the Athenians down even to the time of Demetrius Phalereus, for they took away the old planks as they decayed, putting in new and stronger timber in their places, insomuch that this ship became a standing example among the philosophers, for the logical question of things that grow; one side holding that the ship remained the same, and the other contending that it was not the same.
>
> — Plutarch, Theseus

Heraclitus attempted to address this question by considering a river. At different times, we can step into the same river, but the water we encounter each time is not the same water as previously. Is it the same river?

"We both step and do not step in the same rivers. We are and are not.

— Heraclitus

The population of our chapter house changes continuously. Is it still the same after every brother has been replaced?

Perhaps the answer, as Heraclitus posited, is both yes, and no.

At any given time, the current occupants make up the chapter house.

In the view of the MIT housing system, the building, along with the set of brothers residing there at the moment, constitutes the fraternity.

It's a completely different group than when I was there. In Heraclitus' terms, I am not part of that fraternity.

But everyone who's gone through the house is part of a connected stream of brothers. We all make up the Lambda Phi chapter. We all are a part of that fraternity.

Without an unbroken supply of water, a river dries up and ceases to exist. Without new planks, a ship eventually decays.

The chapter's success is our success.

And likewise, the success of every one of the brothers *is* the success of the chapter.

●

It's human nature to compare. As all of us found out early on at MIT, there's always someone smarter. I recently found out from our alumni discussion group that my SAT scores were on the lower end of the range from the brothers in the house.

At that time, I didn't feel that I was less intelligent than most of the other brothers in the house, but then again, maybe that's indicative of someone less intelligent—a total lack of awareness.

But there's always going to be someone smarter in the house, someone who's better in just about any area of expertise or endeavor. We will not be as successful, in business, or any other endeavors, as many of our alumni brothers.

That's a given. In an email thread, Brother Jeff Foley put it this way:

Whenever you thought you were good at something, there was always someone better. Not just obnoxiously better, but admirably so. As well as a realization that you could spend the rest of your life focusing on how to get as good as they were now, and you might never get there, let alone survive the rest of your responsibilities.

We hear about fraternity success stories, but we generally don't hear anything regarding non-successes. So, any comparisons we make to other brothers are always biased towards making our achievements look less than stellar.

We can only be who we are, and that's something over which we have less control than we might think.

•

Brother Rob Mandel expressed to me that, compared to the many success stories, it's easy for him to feel like one of the "non-successes." As I stated earlier, I can relate.

Several years ago, Rob visited Thailand on a personal pilgrimage. He met an abbot who asked for a donation. Rob said "Certainly," and offered him a cash gift.

"Don't give it to me, give it to my students who need money for books, uniforms, bus fare."

So, Rob sent $500, then $1000, and later $2000 for students to attend school. Eventually, he decided to formalize his charitable giving and create a non-profit organization for this cause.

The organization set some rules for the money's use.

They had to commit to using the money for school, they needed to continue to respect the Thai culture, and teachers had to visit students at home to verify the funds were used appropriately.

Over time, through his donations and organization, Rob was able to fund thousands of students' educations with his efforts.

Each child sends him a letter with their status. He has hundreds, if not thousands of them. Here's just one sample:

Date 13th August 2008

Dear Dr. Robert Mandel,
    My name is Supattra   . My nickname Tuk.
I was born on July 1991. My family is only 5 people.
My father and Mother both died. Now my brother and I
stay with my grandmother.
    Thank you very much for my scholarship
I will concentrate on learning and use the money
wisely. I wish you have much happiness.

                Sincerely yours,
                Miss. Supattra

It's hard to think of a much better definition of success.

Appendix

Just because I could, and the fact that it seemed like a pretty interesting exercise, I ran excerpts from the book's text through the GPT-3 third-generation language prediction model to see what kinds of prose emerged from the current state-of-the-art. The model uses deep learning to produce human-like text.

I used the shortlyai.com website, which has a GPT-3 license, and which provided the interface geared toward allowing the system to finish writing samples.

I provided the model with an overall description of this book, including the name of our chapter and fraternity, then provided the excerpts from selected sections, and pressed the button.

I was not disappointed. I ran most of the excerpts through quite a few times, and then I picked out the completion I liked best for each excerpt.

A portion of the original text that was fed to the algorithm is shown in bold. The remainder of the text came from GPT-3. I've included my annotation on each.

●

The opening of the book was the obvious place to start. There were quite a few 'alternate histories' to choose from. This one left us particularly triumphant.

> **We stared out into the Killian court at the crowd of freshmen, waiting for Dr. Weisner to say, "the words."**
>
> **We'd carved out a small stake on the grassy periphery of the court, battling for prime real estate with thirty other MIT fraternities. Standing ground on our patch of turf, a few things set us apart from the other groups of fraternity brothers gathered around us.**
>
> We wore a uniform—unique jackets for each chapter. Our members had a distinct, recognizable look from which we could build our identity and express our pride. And we were not the only ones with that identity—we were not the only fraternity at MIT.
>
> Dr. Weisner's voice rang out over the crowd: "Alpha Delta Phi invites the best men in America to join Lambda Phi!" The rush began immediately, and soon forty-three members had gotten up on their knees and begun chanting: "All hail Alpha Delta Phi!"
>
> The other groups scattered, leaving us alone at our pedestal in the middle of the court.

•

I liked this addition to the trophy-stealing story because it turned the narrative from a humorous description of events into a scene from a horror movie.

> **...they saw the source of light that had led them into this place.**
>
> **It was a large number ten commercial food can, with a flame burning brightly from the wick in its center.**
>
> **It smelled like bacon.**
>
> The thieves stood and watched the can. Nervously, they took a step closer.
>
> "We should run," whispered one.

They were going to argue further when a voice interrupted them from behind. It was very soft at first, but it grew louder until it was booming in their ears.

"I was wondering where you two had gotten to!"

A third figure appeared next to the can of bacon grease. He wore an all-white chef's uniform with tall chef hat and thick gloves that reached all the way up to his elbows.

The man in the uniform grinned wickedly as he raised a butcher knife above his head and took a half step toward them.

•

In this excerpt, GPT-3 saw fit to make some interesting assumptions about Rob's former lifestyle.

> **Rob claims that being head of the Cambridge chapter of the AFL-CIO was extremely helpful to his resume. In a short time, his underground money-laundering scheme made him the richest person in the frat, and soon brought in enough money to buy additional washers and dryers, teaching him a valuable economics lesson:**
>
> "As long as there was dirty laundry in need of laundering, the cash would keep rolling in."
>
> Brother Mandel's college career was nearing its end, and he faced a crossroads; he could either enter "the real world" with his newly acquired financial skills or continue with a life of "booze, broads, and bling-bling."

•

I included this one because GPT-3 picked out a Spock quote that was in some ways better than the one I chose.

> ...
>
> **Comprehension gradually replaced puzzlement. "Asbestos cork, I get it," he said, now chuckling as his mind pictured scenes of jet flames erupting from Uri's**

posterior. "We certainly don't want any ass-flamers."

I watched as he crossed off the name in his ledger, destroying one student's dreams of a new life, while simultaneously preserving the dreams of the rest of us.

I was not sad.

As Mr. Spock would put it so eloquently, a few years later:

"Suffering is seldom productive."

•

In this example, the toilet-throwing incident has been turned into an action-adventure film, concluding with a statement that was eerily appropriate to MIT men.

...

The first throw landed on a pile of loose debris, which absorbed most of the shock of impact. To the dismay of the toilet tossing trio, the toilet survived, nearly intact.

There was only one course of action that reasonable people facing this situation must take.

The second toilet was hurled to the side, landing on a pickup truck parked on the street. The magic of motion picture and sound recording captured every glorious detail of the destruction.

The sound of shattering ceramic was accompanied by a torturous screech as metal crumpled beneath the weight of 900 pounds of porcelain and feces. The sickening crunching noise made by human bone when it collides with solid objects can not truly be reproduced by any man-made medium.

Urine-soaked trousers hit the ground moments later, revealing the pathetic state that men become when they are denied their freedom for too long...

•

In the nude exercise story, the worker's response seems extremely reasonable, and the last line summarizes the futility of so many of us.

> At some point in the summer, the contractors approach us with an "issue." One of the female boarders living in the rear section has a habit of doing nude exercises in her room every morning.
> Attention is paid. We are very intrigued.
> "So, what's the problem?"
> "The workers aren't getting any work done whiles she's... performing. It's becoming a schedule risk."
> "Wait... so you want us to send her to the back of the building? Would that help?"
> The man laughed. "No, no, it'd be better if you could just tell her she needs to stop doing those exercises or we can only make half our plans for the day."
> "I'm not sure how to get a naked woman's attention," I said.

●

This GPT-3 description of the unrenovated house is simply much better than anything I have ever written and is surprisingly accurate to boot.

> ...
> "Good luck," they said, smiling, as they drove away.
> Only one small problem—there was (almost) nothing inside. No furniture, no dining room tables or chairs. No dining room. No dishes, silverware, or glasses. There was nothing to cook with.
> A single, rusting refrigerator sat alone in the cavernous kitchen, ruminating on its own fragility.
> The building's heating system was broken. The walls were cracked and crumbling. Ceilings were stained with water damage, and some rooms were entirely strewn with garbage left behind by those who had lived there before we got there. The bathroom fixtures had been ripped from the walls, and construction refuse littered the floors.

We'd been given a "gift" that came with over sixteen thousand square feet of problems.

•

The last GPT-3 completion I've included seems to suggest that pledging a fraternity is the start of some sort of Faustian bargain. The only question is—how did it know?

...

"What, do I look like some sort of beer-guzzling jock?" he thought, almost loud enough for Fern to hear.

She could see Tom had a bit of an attitude. But then, she kind of liked men with attitudes.

"Fraternities here are different from other colleges," she added, "They're all filled with smart people, and they're a big part of the housing solution. It might be a good alternative for you."

Tom didn't look convinced, so he decided to check it out.

When the bus dropped him off at a large house in the north side of campus, Tom was surprised to see that his new schoolmates seemed... nice.

As he sat down at the dinner table, awaiting the delicacies promised to him by Al Mink, Tom started to rethink his opinion of fraternities.

And later, after seeing a whole houseful of really smart people with neat haircuts and friendly smiles, Tom decided he actually wanted one.

"Yeah sure" he said to Al with a smile. "I'm in – where do I sign?"

Al smiled back.

Made in the USA
Middletown, DE
28 September 2021